MANSPOTTING

Chronicles of Mid-life Romance

Ritu Bhatia

SPEAKING
TIGER

SPEAKING TIGER PUBLISHING PVT. LTD
4381/4, Ansari Road, Daryaganj,
New Delhi-110002, India

First published by Speaking Tiger in paperback 2018

Copyright © Ritu Bhatia 2018

ISBN: 978-93-87693-06-7
eISBN: 978-93-87164-91-8

The moral right of the author has been asserted.

Typeset in Arno Pro by SÜRYA, New Delhi
Printed at Thomson Press India Ltd.

All rights reserved.
No part of this publication may be reproduced, transmitted,
or stored in a retrieval system, in any form or by
any means, electronic, mechanical, photocopying,
recording or otherwise, without the prior
permission of the publisher.

This book is sold subject to the condition that it shall not, by
way of trade or otherwise, be lent, resold, hired out,
or otherwise circulated, without the publisher's
prior consent, in any form of binding
or cover other than that in
which it is published.

A microbiologist by training, **Ritu Bhatia** left the laboratory to pursue a career as a journalist and writer. She was the Delhi editorial representative for *Femina* magazine, editor of *Bride & Home* magazine, and editor of *Good Health*, a weekly supplement published by the *Mail Today* newspaper. Her features, columns, and editorials on health, medicine and women have appeared in *Harper's Bazaar*, *Outlook* magazine, *Hindu Business Line*, *The Indian Express*, *Mail Today*, *Deccan Herald* and *Elle* magazine. Her short stories have been anthologized and published in *Wasafiri*, *Cosmopolitan* and *Imprint* magazine. She has participated in national and international health forums as a jury member, speaker, reporter and trainer, and undertakes consultancies for agencies like UNICEF, The Bill and Melinda Gates Foundation, OXFAM and Save the Children.

*For my mother Pramilla
who believed I was destined
to be prime minister*

Contents

Introduction	ix
1. Hanging on to My Chastity Belt	1
2. Life as a Wife	9
3. Starting from Scratch	18
4. Finding a Room of My Own	25
5. Love, Again	32
6. Entering the World of Middle-aged Singles	40
7. Dating Mores According to the Experts	48
8. Conversations Over Coffee	55
9. Married and on the Make	71
10. Mr Middle-aged and His Mummy Are Never Parted	100
11. The World of HIV and Intellectual Men	123
12. Bad Boys, Bad Boys What You Gonna Do	137
13. Metamorphosis into a Desi Cougar	165
14. A Close Shave	182
15. A New Beginning	202

Introduction

A strange thing happened when I started living alone in my late thirties. My newly single status turned me into a magnet for middle-aged ladies looking to strike out on their own. The editor of a women's magazine I freelanced for began complimenting me on my appearance, making statements like, 'Your skin is absolutely glowing,' or 'You must be working out a lot these days.'

One day, she invited me to lunch at Bercos. I happily accepted, not imagining for a second that she had an ulterior motive. The chicken spring rolls had just arrived when she began her inquisition.

'So tell me all about it—what it's like being single at your age?' she said, dipping a piece delicately into soya sauce.

I stared at the bits of stuffing that fell out of my own disintegrating roll for a few seconds, and tried to summon up an upbeat, enthusiastic response. Fortunately Ms Editor jumped in to fill the silence. 'Couldn't be easy to find a nice guy, right?' she ventured, with raised eyebrows.

Her presumption goaded me into saying what I did next. 'Oh, there are *plenty* of eligible middle-aged guys around,' I said confidently. 'In fact I'm spoiled for choice.'

Ms Editor dropped her soup spoon in surprise. When a mutual friend told me later that the lady was in the throes of a messy divorce, our lunchtime conversation began to make sense.

Another time, Leena—whose daughters were in school

with my son, and whom I barely knew—cornered me after a PTA meeting. She had an eager, expectant look on her face. 'I really need to talk to you, Ritu,' she whispered, 'to get your advice about something.'

I was surprised, since I'd never spoken to her before. Why would she want *my* advice about anything at all?

'I'm thinking about getting a divorce. But I'm worried whether I will be able to make a fresh start for myself,' she said, in a tremulous voice. 'What do you think?'

I took a deep breath, aghast at being put in the position of saying something potentially disastrous, something that could be thrown back at me at a later date. *You said it would work out, now look at me. You never told me about the shit that would come flying my way... where ARE all the nice guys?*

'Umm...well...I'm not sure what you mean by a fresh start,' I muttered, trying to steer the conversation in a more innocuous direction. 'Maybe you should talk to an expert, a professional counsellor... you know, a person qualified to guide you.'

But Leena wasn't about to let me off so easily. 'No, no, I don't need a professional. I just want to know how things have been for you...whether there are any eligible single men of our age around...what my chances of my finding romance again are...of getting remarried?'

On the one hand, it was flattering being regarded as a mentor for women miserable in their marriages, and keen on finding new love. But I was no relationship guru, and two years of living by myself didn't qualify me to advise anyone: I had nothing worthwhile to say about how well a middle-aged single woman would fare in the urban jungle of romantic relationships.

My failure to settle down in a marriage, and more recent decision to end a potentially long-term romantic relationship, had led me to question all my assumptions about love. I had no idea where to start looking for a suitable romantic partner, and was equally confused about whether I wanted a permanent relationship or not.

∼

A decade later, I had lots to say about mid-life dating and romance. I could tell Leena about what kind of love life she, and other women of my age, could anticipate. Some of it was clichéd, and involved all the stuff everyone knew: that single women of a certain age are considered easy game by men; that the pool of middle-aged men who are good relationship material is small; that the chances of remarriage get slimmer with every year, and so on. Indeed, middle-aged liaisons are fraught with uncertainty.

But the other side of the picture was more interesting. This was about changing social mores, flexible dating rules, and navigating romance in a society beset with contradictions and judgments about right and wrong when it comes to women's sexual and romantic behaviour. Finding my way in the New World of relationships was an exasperating, and sometimes painful experience. My curious and gullible nature was both a blessing and a hazard.

I grew up in the 70s. Courtship rules were black-and-white. You met someone for the first time, face to face. You talked over the phone—there were no emails or text messages to help you escape conversation. Men led the way in courtship, women responded, and if things worked out well, you got married and had babies. But somewhere along the way, all this changed. New, flexible Rules for Love, Sex and Dating evolved, and romance acquired blurred edges. Everyone seemed to be bumbling along, making up new moves. Online dating became popular, and the digital era transformed communication: love letters were replaced by messages on Facebook walls, and texting took over from phone conversations. A sliding morality crept in, making it hard to attribute any significance to emotional or sexual intimacy. Romantic relationships were tinged with uncertainty.

Re-entering the world of singletons as a middle-aged woman was scary, because I was stuck in the muddled space between the old world and the new. *Manspotting: Chronicles of Mid-life Romance* is a memoir that chronicles some of my romantic experiences during this phase of my life. Like every other woman I know, I believed that happiness depended upon finding Mr Right. Embarking upon a mid-life journey to find him was an act of optimism, and sharing some slices of my experiences is an act of bravery.

Since it's impossible to tell the whole story, what follows are some tales of that time, chosen to highlight my delusions, obsessions and triumphs. The stories are true, but names, dates and certain identifying characteristics of people and incidents in this book have been altered to protect privacy.

1
Hanging on to My Chastity Belt

I was a novice in the department of love, relationships and sex when I married in my early twenties. The closest I'd come to having sex before I married, was close dancing to Donna Summer's 'Love to Love You Baby' at sneaky afternoon parties held in homes empty of parents, with the curtains drawn to darken the room. I was sixteen years old, part of a gang of girls studying at St Joseph's Convent in Nagpur. Our secret ambition was to cozy up to the Class X boys of St Francis' school. By the time the Bee Gees released 'How Deep Is Your Love', our hormones were raging, and we were hell bent on finding our soulmates on the dance floor. Seduction began and ended with the music. The formula for romance was simple: *Boy meets girl, they fall in love, marry and live happily ever after.*

My preoccupation with love began much earlier though, at the age of twelve, when my family relocated from Mumbai to Zambia, in Africa. This move was prompted by my dad's job. I joined the International School of Lusaka, and spent the first few months adjusting to the mind-boggling freedom in my new school. Dire Straits played during recess, and the tuck shop sold chocolates and hot dogs. On the last Friday of every month, the school held 'socials', where boys and girls mingled freely, flirting and setting up movie dates.

But I was an Indian girl, and my parents' rules for me

differed from those of my Swedish, American and German classmates. The Rules didn't permit unsupervised outings with pals, or participation in school socials.

'Absolutely not,' was my parents' response, when I pleaded with them to let me join my classmates at these events. 'Focus on your studies,' commanded my dad.

My classmates were curious about my absence, and rumours about my parents' regressive Indian rules began spreading, to my detriment.

'You're just a curry-muncher!' one particularly nasty British boy threw at me. I hated being different, but my parents weren't worried about the social ostracism.

They were more concerned about perpetuating what they called 'Indian culture and values.' Purity is the chief virtue of Indian women, my dad emphasized. Boys were dangerous, and not to be trusted since their main intention was to stake a claim to a girl's virginity. They had the potential to ruin our lives.

Still, I couldn't help developing a crush on a senior, Mark W. He was a gangly American, with an alluring habit of flipping his golden-brown hair back, when it fell into his hazel-green eyes. Between classes, and during recess, I hung around the corridors of our school, lusting after him and thinking up ways to attract his attention.

My mother, who was a teacher in the nursery section of the school, picked up on my obsession. She thwarted Mission Mark by insisting I spend my break time in the school library, reading George Orwell's *Animal Farm*. I was devastated at being separated from Mark, and expressed my revolt by sneakily watching the detective series *Mannix* and *Mission Impossible* while my parents were at dinner parties, and my sisters lay in slumber. Unsupervised TV viewing was almost a crime in our home.

To make my rebellion more impactful, I munched Perugina Baci chocolates stolen from my dad's desk, during these sessions. Before sleeping, I stood mournfully before the bathroom mirror, crooning Roberta Flack's song 'Killing Me Softly':

Strumming my pain with his fingers
Singing my life with his words
Killing me softly with his song
Killing me softly with his song
Telling my whole life with his words
Killing me softly with his song

～

The Rules remained unchanged when we moved back to India, to the small town of Nagpur. By then, I was a plump 15-year-old, lovestruck by B, a guy who played tennis at the local club. He was muscular and fair-skinned, with a sharp nose and an attitude of disdain. He ignored me, making his preference for the slim, long-haired girls who went swimming with him obvious. It took six months of pining and dieting to get him to notice me.

B was my first boyfriend. We met secretly, slow-danced at parties, kissed and cuddled and conducted long conversations over the phone. Since those were the days of landlines, my sisters picked up the extension whenever they could, and overheard our chats. Once in a while, they threatened to expose our love affair to my parents.

But before they could carry out their threat, my father

was posted to Chandigarh. We moved to a large bungalow near Sukhna Lake, and I joined the Government College for Girls. My father decided that I should become a doctor: it was such a noble profession! But I was unconvinced, and refused to study for the medical college exams. When I failed, dad marched me along to the department of biosciences at Panjab University, and asked me to choose between biophysics, biochemistry or microbiology. A cursory glance at the brochure painted an exciting future for microbiologists: the beer and cheese industry relied on microbes, as did cutting-edge medical technologies. I could easily envision myself flitting around in a pristine white lab coat, peering into a vat of beer or discovering a cure for cancer.

So, at the age of eighteen, I found myself at the Department of Microbiology in Panjab University. Here too, the Rules remained in place. *If you sleep with him, you'll have to marry him,* was the updated version. So I stayed away from boys, and developed intense relationships with the bacteria I viewed through the microscope instead: *Entamoeba histolytica, lactobacillus acidophilus, Salmonella Typhi.* My evenings were spent keeping company with bacterial cultures in Petri dishes.

While most other girls my age were tearing around town on the back of their boyfriends' motorcycles, I had the privilege of riding around on my own red Hero Honda Luna. Somehow, I had managed to persuade my dad how important it was for me to own a set of wheels. He agreed, reluctantly. The deal was that I had to wear a helmet. I honoured it, till I turned the corner from our house and reached the main road. After that I'd take it off in relief: I hated the weight on my head, and felt stupid wearing the bulky thing on my motorized cycle, which had a maximum speed of 40 kmph.

At home I was granted special privileges: being a science student exempted me from doing household chores. I had no idea how to make a bed, poach an egg, or pour tea from a teapot without sloshing it all over the tray. Though I interacted with a handful of guys in my department, close or frequent encounters with males were taboo, unless they served a specific purpose. The only boy I saw on a regular basis was Sukhi, short for Sukhwinder. He was the garrulous son of a neighbour, who studied engineering at the local college.

My father took him up on his offer to help me with maths and physics. So I had to suffer Sukhi's monotonous voice three evenings a week. Admittedly he explained Newton's laws of motion really well, but I was distracted by the wispy hairs of his moustache which fell into his mouth when he spoke. It amazed me how oblivious Sukhi was to his own lack of charm, and how he blustered on confidently. At the end of the lesson, he made neat notations in black ink on my notebook, underlining sentences and paragraphs. 'This is your homework,' he said authoritatively.

I nodded frantically, desperate to be rid of him, and go for my driving lessons. These were conducted by my father, who accompanied me with his shaving mirror, used to monitor the traffic behind. I navigated our Ambassador car clumsily around the neighbourhood, often losing control of the wheel, zigzagging on the road and rolling onto pavements. I even slammed into the gatepost of our house once, but to my relief, this didn't put a stop to the driving lessons, by far the most exciting activity of my life at the time.

~

The other male visitor to our house was a cherubic collegemate, Manish, who had a reputation for his 'green fingers'. It was obvious that he had a crush on me. He met my father at a college meeting, and offered to prune the roses in our garden. Sure enough, he showed up at the house with his giant shears one morning and snipped away at the bushes. The plants, however, refused to flower. But Manish brushed off this failure, blaming the manure used on the plants for their death. He wooed me even more fiercely after this incident, placing a daily beaker full of seasonal flowers he had supposedly grown himself, at my workstation in the laboratory: gardenias, sweetpeas, narcissi and roses, which exuded a heady perfume and incited a great deal of teasing from my classmates.

His frank expression of interest in me was both flattering and irritating. I pined for other, more elusive guys in the university: Sammy with the dimples who studied in the men's college next door; the tall, athletic Aviraj in the chemical engineering department; and Ravneet with his sparkling eyes, in the MBA department. I fixated on one at a time, and proceeded to expend an extraordinary amount of time trying to gain his attention.

Ultimately, Aviraj and I had a short-lived, clandestine romance involving desperate meetings in park corners, sneaky phone conversations, and an exchange of love letters. This liaison fizzled out almost as quickly as it began. Hanging on to my hymen was no easy matter, and the threat of being forced to marry him or any other guy I fancied—just because I had broken the Rules—was too ominous. Also, my academic schedule didn't leave much time for romantic pursuits.

~

Achievement was the name of my game. I was in the college swimming and debating team, and an active participant in declamation contests. Medals and certificates hung on the walls of my bedroom. The names and characteristics of bacteria and parasites floated through my mind day and night: *Clostridium tetani, Plasmodium vivax, Naegleria fowleri.* They danced in and out, like verse.

My life's mission was to learn about their special characteristics—the conditions in which they flourished, and withered. My MSc thesis topic was to prove that the persistent nature of the bug *Escherichia coli* (E.coli) was linked to its tendency to stick to cells. To prove this point, I had to dissect a rat a day.

Every morning, I accompanied the smirking lab assistant to the animal house, and we chose our victim together, from the dozens scrambling about in a giant cage. We doused a wad of cotton with chloroform to anaesthetize the black, furry creature. By the time the rat was pinned on its back on a wax slab, my eyes watered and my nose dripped. The kidneys I teased out of the creature appeared shrunken and forlorn. My scientific world made me sick.

My sanctum away from the laboratory was my bedroom, more specifically my bed, where I sat propped up on my pillows, reading James Hadley Chases' and Mills and Boon romances and *Cosmopolitan* magazines, borrowed from the Sector 8 market lending library. The world inhabited by the heroes and heroines in the novels and magazines was so racy and colourful, so far-removed from my own narrow, analytical one.

I flipped the pages of *Cosmopolitan* and fantasized about becoming a femme fatale with purple lipstick, dressed in skimpy clothes, and seated on a plush white sofa. Maybe one day I would appear on the cover of *Vogue*, or get a part in a romantic TV show?

A tall, good-looking man hovered somewhere in the picture, though I can't recall his distinguishing characteristics. I played and re-played Paul Anka's sexist song, 'You're having my baby', all evening, convinced that getting pregnant was the ultimate expression of love.

At twenty-two, my notions of love were hazy. My mother and father had had a love marriage, and so had their brothers and sisters. The disgruntlement amongst certain members of the family over these unions was a topic of hot discussion, and I especially enjoyed the tale of an aunt who was bold enough to elope with the man she had decided to marry. My own romantic future was abundant with possibilities.

•

2
Life as a Wife

I met my future husband, G, when I was just thirteen years old. Our parents were friends, almost relatives, in fact, since G's father's sister was married to my dad's maternal uncle. G and his parents lived in Washington, and we met each other for the first time during a family holiday to the US. My parents, sisters and I stayed at their place for a few days.

I caught just a few glimpses of G, who was a shy, bearded man with a soft voice. I sneaked around his bedroom when he was away at college, curiously touching the cardboard models of buildings clustered on his desk, and peering at his books on Bauhaus. At that time, he was studying architecture; and I was in school in Lusaka.

Tragedy struck G's family, not long after we met in Washington. His father passed away prematurely, and his mother moved back to Delhi. But G continued living in the US. I was twenty-one when we met again. Then, I had just embarked on my MSc degree, and he had returned to settle in India, after a twenty-year stint outside.

He and his widowed mother were in Chandigarh, for a family wedding. I was attracted to his enigmatic, humorous personality, and sat self-consciously beside him in my parents' drawing room. At the time, I was madly in love with T, the F&B manager of a coffee shop in a five-star hotel. But my father refused to accept T, on the basis that we weren't suitably matched.

'What kind of life will you have with a hotelier?' he demanded.

Standing up to my dad was too much work, so I capitulated, after a brief show of resistance. In retrospect, I must have had my own doubts about the feasibility of my union with T. By this stage, I was also tired of struggling with my romantic impulses, which seemed destined to be quashed just as soon as they arose.

∽

Weeks later, the possibility of pairing with G arose. It began with a knock on the bathroom door. I peered out in alarm. My father stood outside in his pajamas, holding a newspaper, which he kept thrusting in my face.

'You must read G's article—it's excellent!'

'Can't I even go to the bathroom in peace!' I yelled, banging the door shut. Secretly, I was excited at the prospect of a romantic involvement with G. He was much older, experienced, and had lived most of his life in the US. In my imagination, Indian men with a Western education were more liberated in their views, and more supportive of women's independence.

I decided I may as well get married. What else could I do anyway? My father's suggestion that I enroll in some fancy Western university and pursue a higher education in the sciences didn't appeal to me at all. By now, the lack of fun in my life was glaring. I longed to shed my serious demeanour and get a life outside the laboratory, and my bedroom. Surely I had a right to the frivolous concerns of a young woman my age? For as long as I could recall, my life had been lived in my head, and I was poised for a new beginning. I dreamt of dancing, travel and lovemaking.

Six months later, G and I were engaged. Since I still had to finish my MSc thesis, our marriage was postponed for another six. During this period, we wrote letters to each other. He came to visit me in Chandigarh, and I made a few visits to Delhi. It was all very romantic, but our meetings were brief, and didn't help us get to know each other any better. In retrospect, I am flabbergasted by the facile manner in which I made the decision to marry. I hadn't really thought about what kind of love, or life, I wanted. Perhaps this was because I'd never had the opportunity to discover my own interests and aspirations. For twenty-two years, I had lived based on a script written by others.

~

Like most other Indian women of my generation, I made a jailbreak marriage, moving directly from my father's home to my husband's. From being a naïve, gauche college student with a restricted life, I was thrust into a joint family, with a husband, mother-in-law and grandmother-in-law. My husband was highly cerebral, with an interest in architecture, arts and journalism.

In the typical way of intellectuals, he was lost in his own world of ideas. Like me, his decision to marry had been almost offhand, motivated more by his desire to settle down to life in India, than his keenness to be a husband. Marriage was part of a new plan, made by both of us, almost carelessly. We really hadn't envisaged the adjustments required to make our union flourish.

Life as a wife and daughter-in-law was as far removed as possible from the fantasy I'd created in my head. Marriage is no safe haven for many women in India. A married woman is supposed to take on the traditional roles of a wife and daughter-in-law, the moment she steps into her new home. A husband is the closest an Indian wife can get to god, and caring for him is her primary duty. Her other responsibilities include managing the mundane aspects of his life—wardrobe, food, social connections—so that he is free to pursue his work in the world outside.

A wife, I discovered, also has household chores, which include the supervision of maids and cooks, and keeping the house in perfect running order—the polishing of furniture, regular changing of linen, grocery shopping and meal planning. Of course, the major-domo of all operations is the mother-in-law. Regardless of how outwardly 'modern' a family appears, social traditions and customs are rigidly ingrained in the psyche of older Indian women who become mothers-in-law, and dictate their expectations from their daughters-in-law. In the end, a woman's adaptation to a joint family depends upon how well she responds to her mother-in-law's control.

In general, women in an Indian society are lauded more for their willingness to adjust and adapt to often unsavoury situations, than for their intellect and talents. Unselfishness and 'good deeds' generate a great deal of praise: 'She gets up at 6 a.m. to make sure the kids get a good breakfast,' or 'She takes her mother-in-law to the temple every day,' or 'She makes sure her husband's clothes are perfectly coordinated.'

The conspiracy hatched by society to mould women

into creatures devoted to the service of others has been the downfall of many dreams. I've watched the signature strengths of my talented classmates—brilliant research abilities, expert managerial qualities, exceptional athletic skills—dissipate slowly, while concerns about children, in-laws and maidservants take precedence.

I too struggled with the role cast on me by the collective: that of decorative wallpaper in my husband's life.

'So what's your husband up to these days?' was a question thrown at me, by men and women alike, on social occasions.

'No idea,' I'd retort curtly, 'why don't you ask him yourself?'

It struck me as odd that most never inquired about what work I was occupied with, or my view on anything of significance—a world event, a painting, a book or movie, a discovery. Though I had a Master's degree, just like G, and both of us published articles in the papers regularly, people in our circle inevitably brought up his work. Mine was dismissed as a hobby.

~

I was totally unprepared for the dynamics of joint-family life. I was only twenty-two, a novice in the art of housekeeping, with no idea how to relate intimately to a man, leave alone his mother and grandmother.

Having been raised in an atmosphere where my academic achievements counted above domestic skills, I had no housekeeping talents to rely upon. The pressure of trying to transform overnight from a college student to a married woman was paralyzing. I was perplexed by the failure of my education and upbringing to prepare me for this situation. None of my major successes so far—getting E.coli to stick to rat kidney cells, winning swimming competitions, and mastering the steering wheel of the cantankerous Ambassador car—amounted to much in my new life.

I couldn't cook, had no idea how to go ration shopping, or how long clothes had to be soaked in detergent before they were washed. Socially, too, I was ill-suited to the demands of family life. My brooding temperament and outspoken manner offended everyone. I was poor at the small talk required to keep daily relationships running smoothly.

My spirits sagged when I stepped outside my bedroom into the company of domestics, in-laws, and numerous others who came and went. The social fabric of Indian married life is tempered with endless interactions, which most women have grown up with, and are used to. But my existence had led me to develop a natural inclination for solitude, and I found it hard to respond to so many people and situations.

Many years later, I learned about Jung's theory of psychological types, through a corporate buddy who was forced to take a test devised to assess his personality type. Called the Briggs-Myer Type Indicator, he said it provided him new and useful insights into his behaviour.

'Here's a copy for you,' he said enthusiastically, pulling out a folder from his briefcase. The Briggs-Myer classification of personalities explains how variations of behaviour in healthy people are a result of our inborn tendencies to use our minds differently. Quirky behaviour for one person maybe normal for another, yet this very difference tends to become a source of great misunderstanding.

Despite my skepticism, I sat down and took the test. I fell into the INFJ category, 'Introverted Intuition with Extraverted Feeling.' This category of person is intense, intuitive but also extremely closed and private. Though they value connections, they also need time alone in order to thrive. When I read this, my breath stilled. In the list of stressors for INFJ-type people was 'dealing with details, especially things in the outer world' and 'too much extraverting.' This rung so true, that it almost hurt.

⁓

My career was also on shaky ground. My training as a microbiologist was useless, since I couldn't overcome my revulsion for the colourless, sterile environment of a laboratory, which had surfaced during my student days. Attempts to create an alternative work life as a freelance journalist, writing features on health and women's issues for magazines and newspapers, didn't provide the gratification or income of a solid profession.

Though I enjoyed writing, I lacked the drive to make it a full-time profession. Occasional sparks of creativity prompted me to write short stories, which found their way into magazines like *Debonair* and *Imprint*, and even some international journals. Some were included in anthologies, and shortlisted for literary prizes. But my demons stalled my writing, never allowing it to take center stage in my life. I lost interest in my plot, too early.

Though everyone waited for me to have a baby, I was

conflicted about motherhood. The thought of having to give up my time alone, and surrender to the demands of a child, was frightening. Though I was conditioned to believe that mothering came naturally to women (since they were biologically designed for childbearing), I wasn't convinced about this. I knew very little about feminism, yet couldn't help feeling that having a child to look after would restrict my freedom.

Still, the birth of my son, L, was probably the most joyous event of my life. The emotional connection I forged with him was both unexpected and thrilling. I fell passionately in love with my baby, even though I lacked the patience mothers need for the routine chores involved in childcare. Despite my disinclination towards domestic work, I was keen to bring up L myself, and hovered around the maids who helped look after him.

Yet, I resisted becoming a Tiger Mother, the famous term coined by writer Amy Chua. I had friends who had turned neurotic as a result of their struggle to sublimate their ambition and professional drive into controlling their children. They expended every ounce of their physical and mental energy on mothering, supervising their kids' meals, sleep times, social activities and homework. Micromanagement was their forte, and they lived by their belief that their kids' success would serve as a sparkling reflection of their mothering skills.

My decision to parent L without controlling and directing him was influenced in large part by the school he went to. This was a 'free progress' school, led by educators who were adamant that parents raise children in a conscious manner. Freedom was the basis of their educational philosophy. At every single PTA meeting, the principal would say, 'Learn to trust your children,' to me and the other worried mothers.

This was a scary thought. All the parents I'd ever encountered (including my own) were followers of Dr Benjamin Spock's child-rearing philosophies, and believed in setting rigid rules and regulations for their offspring. Fathers and mothers who didn't try and curb their children's freedom were labelled 'incompetent' and 'lazy'. Finding the balance between hanging on and letting go of L was a challenge.

3

Starting from Scratch

The pleasure I got out of motherhood notwithstanding, my feelings of unhappiness persisted. So I started seeing a counsellor, AD, in my early thirties, in an attempt to find a solution to my misery. AD was a beautiful 50-year-old self-contained single woman who kept a serene home and pursued a range of esoteric interests: Sufism, pottery, Rolfing, craniosacral therapy, and so on. The combination of her calm demeanour and brown leather couch provided me temporary relief from my distress. For the first time in my life, I had the luxury of receiving someone's full attention. She was a good listener, and didn't judge me at all.

With her guidance, I learned to use a therapeutic framework called Transactional Analysis (TA) to understand the dynamics of my behaviour and relationships. Developed by Dr Eric Berne (author of *I'm OK, You're OK*), in the 1960s, this is based on the notion that we have three 'ego-states' that interact with each other in our interactions with others, or 'transactions'. In an ideal interaction, there's no clash between these three ego states. But since most of us are unaware of how these ego states impact our style of communication, we end up with dissatisfactory relationships.

Though considered an antiquated model of therapy today, TA offered me mind-blowing insights into myself, forcing me to examine how my entire demeanour—words, body language and facial expressions—affected my communication. The structured approach of TA appealed to my rational mind more than the other, more common, method used by therapists: that of encouraging a person to talk until the 'problem' and 'solution' emerged.

Most importantly, TA helped me shed the feeling of helplessness I'd grown so familiar with, through its central concept of 'script'. According to Berne, we decide on a well-defined course of action during our childhood, depending on how we experience the world. Instinctively, we make decisions on how we need to act, in order to survive in it. This is reinforced by parental figures and other caregivers. So, we tend to cling onto this childhood pattern of adaptation, even as adults. And we remain stuck, unless we become aware of our script and work towards changing it.

Viewed through this lens, I saw that I had lived my life till now, based largely on other people's expectations. Like other Indian women of my generation, I'd been conditioned to believe that my life should be dedicated to the collective happiness of others. Subconsciously, I had relegated my own pleasure and satisfaction to a junk heap somewhere and was 'surviving', rather than 'thriving'. The sad part was that I had no idea what I liked or wanted, since I'd never been encouraged to either create or follow my own path. Over the years, discounting my own needs had become a habit.

Learning and practicing TA in the safe environment provided by AD, offered me the hope I needed to change this script. Her world view found resonance in mine.

She was an extremely independent person who believed women to be competent and capable of forging their own way in the world. She encouraged me to find strength in myself. Since she valued being truthful, interacting with her taught me the power of telling the truth, at all times. We were similar in our search for silence, strength and self-sufficiency.

Still, my personal excavation frightened me. The gap between the person I'd imagined myself to be, and the one I was now viewing through a magnifying glass, was wider than I had realized. Though I thrived on the thought of family and continuity, my experience revealed that I wasn't built for domestic life. I adored my child, but struggled with the responsibility of mothering. Hanging on to familiar routines and people became harder and harder, as everything about my existence was slippery. By the fifty-second session of examining what I did and didn't do, believed and disbelieved, wanted and didn't want, I was ready for change.

~

My life as I knew it fell apart when I was in my mid-thirties. Not surprisingly, the disintegration in my psyche bred ill-health: I came down with jaundice, and moved back to my old bedroom in my parents' house. I crawled into bed, relieved that my inflamed liver provided me an excuse to evade the questions that arose from all quarters. Facing up to the fact that I was maladjusted to marriage and domestic life, had no deep, satisfying interests, no distinct career path, and no optimistic vision of my future, was gut-wrenching.

Two months later, my bilirubin levels were back to normal. I was five kilos lighter and utterly confused about where to start the journey to a happier version of myself. But what I did know was that unless I made a bid for a new existence, I was destined to be miserable. I could no longer avoid leaving my marital home.

My decision to strike out on my own was greeted with shock and derision by everyone. 'You're going through mid-life adolescent rebellion,' remarked an aunt sarcastically. Women who decide to start afresh in mid-life must face that most friends and family members of the same age are well 'settled' with husbands, kids, in-laws, maids, drivers, chowkidars and dogs. My decision to turn my safe life into an uncertain one, contrasted sharply with the apparently secure and predictable existence of many in my circle, who regarded me as crazy, stupid and selfish.

Go for marriage counselling instead... every child needs both parents... how could you do this... just go on a holiday and you'll feel better...

~

In the mid-90s I became a singleton again. Supporting myself had never struck me as an option in my twenties, and I wasn't sure it was a viable choice for me at this stage of my life. How could I do it anyway? True independence cost money, and I had no idea how to create a substantial, income-generating career. I couldn't imagine myself in a full-time job, since this meant sustaining an interest in an occupation—something I hadn't managed so far. The only real job I'd held was in my capacity as a microbiologist. The experience had left me dispirited, and led me to abandon the possibility of a career in the lab. So, how to earn enough money to pay for my existence?

The answer came sooner than I'd expected, when I ran into Arvind, a flamboyant, twice-divorced acquaintance who had just taken over as the CEO of an American publishing company setting up business in India.

'I've been trying to get hold of you all week,' he said when we met. 'There's a job opening at my office…and I know it's tailormade for you.'

I was surprised when I heard the position he was considering me for was that of a sales manager. How could I possibly even consider accepting it? I had no idea how to sell anything, be it a book or a bar of soap. What was Arvind thinking?

'It'll be a cinch for you, yaar…you know half the city, and all you need to do is get them interested in our books,' he said, brushing aside my misgivings, and offering me a salary large enough to stop me from saying no. Also, he agreed to let me continue my freelance writing career, outside office hours.

~

A week later, I sat at a desk in my new office fiddling with a box of business cards: 'Ritu Bhatia—Sales Manager, BK Books.'

The office was a cheery place. Arvind was a lively employer, who treated me and a couple of female colleagues to lunch at a fancy restaurant every fortnight, regaling us with stories of his ex-wives each time.

'C expects me to send the car and driver to her every day, can you believe it!'…'M says I should pay for her holiday in Europe, since she's raising our child single-handedly'... 'C insists that I visit her mother in hospital, for old time's sakes.'

His current flame was a 25-year-old jewellery model, who kept him on his toes.

'I have one of those trainer fellows to keep my paunch down, yaar—how else to keep up with her!'

Once in a while, Arvind would send me off to run the kind of errand that a boss typically expects from a female employee: shopping for birthday presents and shower curtains. I didn't mind though, since it was more fun picking silk scarves from Christina's than it was selling books.

My job was tougher than I'd imagined. The business model followed by BK Books was similar to that of Tupperware and Avon. Direct marketing via book parties was their sales strategy. As the sales manager, I had to persuade at least 150 people a month to sign up and commit to the business by paying 2,500 rupees to own a set of books, which they were supposed to market through 'book parties', which were basically gatherings of people who ended up becoming customers.

The folks I'd signed up were also supposed to expand their own businesses, by inducing others to become their 'down-lines': these new hires would also invest in a set of books, and proceed to sell books in the same way, passing on some of their profit to the upper tier of people.

But this sounded easier than it was. Inducting this many people into a book business meant I had to make at least fifty calls a day and make endless small talk. Though I enjoyed the occasional socializing, it was depressing to be forced into daily social interaction of this intensity. I found some solace in the articles I continued to write in my free time—it was a relief to do something creative after all the mindless chatter.

4
Finding a Room of My Own

After two years of living with my parents, I decided it was time to strike out on my own. I deliberated the matter of renting my own place with AD. She was convinced I had the resilience required to set up an independent establishment. 'You don't need much,' she said confidently. 'A stove, saucepan, bed and dhurrie.'

Her advice was contrary to everyone else's: *living alone in this city is a bad idea, so unsafe, you'll never make it on your own, what will people say, women like you will never get used to slumming…* Stories about landlords who refused to let properties to single women, and the atrocities suffered by women who lived alone made for grim dinnertime conversation. Despite all the rhetoric about women's rights, single women in the city still weren't ensured acceptance or safety.

At random, I dialled the number of a property agent whose ad I'd spotted in the property pages of the *Times of India*. His name was Rukun and he spoke perfect English, in a deep Amitabh Bachchan baritone, that appealed instantly. I arranged to meet him in his office, which turned out to be a tiny room in a crumbling DDA market, at odds with the baritone and the fragrance of Old Spice which hung in the air.

Rukun was a medium-built man in his mid-thirties, who fiddled compulsively with his moustache while he responded to non-stop telephone calls. Men streamed in and out of his office, and he snapped instructions at them in between the calls.

'Sorry, Ms Bhatia,' he said with a grimace. 'Just give me a few minutes.' I smiled tightly, trying to stay calm despite the anxiety rising in my stomach at the thought of finding a place of my own and fending for myself.

All my life, I had lived in safe and secure family homes, surrounded by others. Would I be able to adjust to being alone? Was it safe to trust this unknown property agent whose number I had dialled on a whim? My wandering thoughts came to a standstill when I spotted a large picture of Rukun in a policeman's outfit, standing beside a big-time politician.

I frowned and turned to him inquiringly. 'Is that you?'

Rukun nodded. 'I was his chief of security,' he said, proudly, '...till I quit two years ago.'

'So how did you get into the property business?' I asked, overcome by an irrational sense of relief.

'Leg injury,' replied Rukun, pushing down on his left thigh. 'Now tell me Ms Bhatia, what kind of property are you looking for?'

I took a deep breath and expelled it slowly. 'What I need is a small apartment, on a small budget.'

Rukun straightened up in his chair and pursed his lips. 'What about your husband?' he asked.

'I'll be living alone,' I responded brusquely, '...though my son will come and go.'

Rukun's expression softened. 'I see,' he said, shifting the pile of papers in front of him to the side. 'In that case, I'll show you some places in the morning.'

~

After a week of looking at dismal living spaces, I spotted a tiny barsati apartment in a cul de sac of Green Park that was more habitable than the others. The elderly landlord and his wife seemed pleasant. How would I get them to give me a lease though? I worried about the single women stories and all the horrible things that could happen to me.

Rukun sensed my apprehension, and tried to ease the situation.

'Don't worry,' he said reassuringly. 'Leave it to me. Just let me handle everything.'

I nodded gratefully, clutching the bundle of notes in my bag which had been carefully saved to make a down payment on the apartment.

'The story will be that your husband is in the Gulf,' Rukun asserted. I sighed in resignation: *How stupid this sounds...what nonsensical tales must a woman tell, just to get a place to live.*

My flat was a dark, two-roomed place on the second floor of a house occupied by a joint family. The landlord, Mr Kapoor, and his wife lived on the ground floor with their married son and family; he was a 70-year-old, mild-mannered man, who spent the day managing his dry-cleaning business, and the evening standing at the gate and staring at the street. Mrs Kapoor was a shrill woman who busied herself bossing everybody around.

Her cooking instructions in Punjabi to her daughter-in-law floated through the vent connecting their kitchen to mine. She marched in and out of her own house, and the apartment of her widowed daughter-in-law that was located just below mine. Mrs Kapoor obviously expected to enjoy the same freedom with me, and tried to barge into my place a few times. But I thwarted her attempts by ignoring the doorbell, and her summons, which were made from the bottom of the flight of stairs. 'Ritu...ah, Ritu...ah,' she bellowed. Eventually, she got the message.

The neighbourhood was a middle-class Punjabi one; loud, messy and colourful. Intrusive neighbours yelled across the street to each other, and stood at windows peering into each other's bedrooms. The garlic and onion smells from the Kapoor's kitchen blew straight up into mine, making me feel nauseous.

~

Every time I walked down the dark staircase into the street, I was aware of the inquisitive stares of the older ladies, and the lascivious looks of their husbands. But everyone was pleasant enough. People I'd never met greeted me enthusiastically, and some of the neighbourhood ladies took to dropping in once in a while.

One of the bestselling titles of BK Books was a dog-training manual, which lay on the back seat of my car. This caught the eye of Rashmi from next door, who had just acquired a Labrador pup. She showed up at my front door one evening. 'Hi, I thought I'd say hello,' she said, looking curiously around the room. 'Do you think I could borrow the book in your car?'

A week after I moved in, I met the Kapoor's vivacious 41-year-old daughter-in-law Smita, who lived in the flat below mine, with her teenage daughter and 22-year-old son. She had been widowed two years earlier, and was frank about the relief she experienced when her husband passed away.

'I was so happy when he died, Ritu,' she confided, clutching my hand as she described the many miserable years she'd spent with her alcoholic husband, who ultimately developed cirrhosis and died of multiple organ failure.

'I was free after a lifetime of being slapped and changing sheets soaked with his pee every morning,' she said.

But a lifetime of being in an unfulfilling romantic and sexual relationship had left Smita yearning for a passionate love affair.

'I want a rishta badly—with sex-vex and all,' she said despairingly, 'Kaise karoon?'

Deep down, Smita knew that she may never free herself from the clutches of her dead husband's family: economic dependence bound her to them, and demanded that she surrender her right to romance and sex. Like other widows in India, she struggled for acceptance from a society discomfited by her presence.

Though widows in families like Smita's are no longer suppressed by regressive customs that force them to don white sarees and remain in isolation, the unspoken expectation of abstinence looms heavy. Remarriage is still more the exception than the norm. And unless widowed women have the financial means, they are doomed to returning to their parental or in-laws' homes, and a life lived at the mercy of family members. In Smita's case, her mother-in-law and son monitored her every movement. Her helplessness was acute.

But she was warm and affectionate towards me, and we took to dropping in on each other, and making trips to the market together for ice-cream. Smita was envious of my independence but couldn't comprehend why I'd chosen to live alone.

'When are you getting married?' she asked often.

'I'm not,' I replied emphatically.

'But at least you should look after your body,' she countered, trying to make light of a situation she didn't understand.

She arranged for the local masseuse, Bubbly—a plump woman who roamed around the neighbourhood carrying a duffel bag with boxes of wax, bleach, creams and other grooming implements—to visit me. Bubbly spent an hour every week, pouring olive oil onto my supine body, and pummelling away.

I was grateful for the temporary distraction Smita provided from my acute loneliness.

~

Since I had no full-time maid in my new apartment, G and I evolved a somewhat unusual and flexible parenting arrangement. Mid-week, I'd leave office at 3 p.m. to pick L up from school, and bring him home to spend the night with me. In addition, he spent weekends with me. The rest of the week, G looked after him.

Mothering a schoolgoing child in my new environment was challenging. Inside, the world closed in on us. Even when I put the lights on, the rooms were dark. Since the flat didn't have the power sanction to run an air conditioner, the heat was sapping. I was emotionally fraught, and often found myself fighting back tears.

Months after G and I had separated, I was forced to sit through a PTA meeting, during which my son's class teacher repeatedly brought up the issue of his 'maladjustment'. She said his new habit of pulling girls' ponytails was an indication of his disturbed emotions.

'Children from broken families are very volatile,' she said, with pursed lips.

The school was one of those spiritually oriented, idealistic places that viewed anything other than a display of sunny emotions, as a red flag. Their laudable commitment to 'morally sound' behaviour managed to make me feel guilty for what they believed to be my child's transgressions. When I chided L for pulling girls' ponytails, he rolled his eyes. 'It was just once, mummy,' he said.

Though L was a model of good behaviour, and had a calm and loving temperament, it didn't stop his teachers and even other parents from making all kinds of unlikely connections between something he had done or said, and his 'turbulent' home life. The implication that I was responsible somehow for everything that went wrong with my child crept into many conversations. I felt miserable and helpless every time I heard this.

5
Love, Again

Change takes time. I had to tell myself this, every single day. Three months after my move to Green Park, instead of feeling happier, I was acutely miserable. Self-doubt crept into my mind: maybe I had been stupid to exchange comfort and stability, for an uncertain future? I forgot about the misery of my previous life, and reminisced instead upon the positive aspects; the walks with G, our trips to the mountains, conversations about books. And the daily home-cooked meals that I'd taken for granted till now.

Though I had some part-time household help, there was no one to buy groceries or cook for me. I had to shop for vegetables and fruit, and prepare my own meals. Despite my gung-ho attitude about living alone, this particular activity was acutely depressing. Sitting down to a hot, freshly prepared meal every night represented nurture to me. Having to cook my own lunch and dinner just didn't feel the same.

Falling madly in love is probably the best distraction from bad feelings. My existential angst was put to rest, temporarily, when I met Vikram at a press conference. While 'beautiful' is a term usually used to describe a woman, that's the word that came to mind when I first saw him: his skin glowed, his shoulders were broad and well-shaped, and he had a perfectly sculpted face. His laughter boomeranged in the spaces he inhabited and his larger-than-life personality made everyone around him seem small and insignificant.

Vikram was the director of an international biotechnology company focused on developing gene-based predictive tests and treatments for all kinds of diseases. It was the beginning of the era of personalized medicine; a couple of years after scientists had mapped the human genome or DNA. The company Vikram worked for was customizing treatments for diseases caused by a single gene mutation, such as sickle cell anaemia and Huntington's disease. 'The right treatment for the right person at the right time' was their tag line.

Perhaps my background in microbiology led to my fascination with the potential of genetics to change the future of medicine. A paper had commissioned me to do a story on the issue, and set up an interview with Vikram. But I hadn't bargained for the effect he would have on me—his good looks threw me off track completely. I found it hard to concentrate on what he said about genes and medicines.

All I could think about was how to avoid meeting his eyes or touching him by mistake. Would he sense how attracted I was to him? I was terrified of being caught out. I needn't have worried though, since the chemistry was mutual. He kept shuffling his papers, changing his position and bursting into inappropriate laughter during our discussion, and by the end of it, we were trapped in a glorious bubble of lust and longing.

A week later he called to suggest lunch. We talked about other articles I could pitch, over tandoori fish at Moet's in

Defence Colony. I made a show of listening, crushed by the wedding ring I had spotted on his finger. All I could really hear was the pounding of my disappointed heart and a reproachful voice in my head: *Did you really expect a man like him to be single?*

I suffered one more long work meeting before I learnt that Vikram was single. He said he wore a wedding ring out of habit, even though his marriage had ended when his wife left him eight months earlier. A divorce was underway, and Vikram was struggling to raise his eight- and ten-year-old sons by himself.

'She didn't want the kids,' he said, sadly. Despite the suggestions of relatives and friends that he put his boys in a boarding school, he was adamant about keeping them at home with him. 'They are my biggest asset,' he insisted.

We fell into a relationship almost naturally. Vikram was passionate about me in the manner of a Mills & Boon hero, plying me with red roses, chocolates and lots of loving attention. I basked in the cocoon of safety and contentment that romance bestows, convinced that Vikram was the Universe's gift to me, miraculous proof that love was life-changing.

He stood before me in all his glory, radiating the vitality and energy that was absent in me and triggering my yearning for life itself. I spent the first few weeks of our relationship gasping for breath, feeling like I was walking on air, and believing that I had only skimmed the surface of emotions till this moment in time.

The only problem was that he wasn't free to be with me in the manner I needed. Managing his high-powered job and young sons was far from easy. Once I got to know him better, I realized how misleading his confident manner was. He struggled to do justice to his role as a single dad, and felt as guilty as a single mother about it. But he was helpless to change the situation, since his job was demanding and involved regular travel.

Meeting his kids' needs was clearly impossible, despite the retinue of maids and drivers he employed. Yet, he refused to consider the possibility of sending them to a residential school.

'They will live with me till they are old enough to do otherwise,' he said emphatically, every time the topic came up.

The boys were sweet and innocent, in the way children are. I was fond of them, in the manner of an aunt, and smiled through kiddie mealtimes and storytelling sessions, though my sense of discomfort was acute. I was stifled by the pressure to respond in a motherly manner, to step in and take over where their birth mother had left off. I told myself that mine was a temporary reaction, which would dissipate over time.

But I couldn't control my expectations of Vikram. I wanted him to be mine, and just mine. I wanted to go to the movies, and dance all night with him. It hurt me that he didn't show up at my front door with containers of hot dal and chicken. After all, he had a cook and driver. Surely it wasn't that hard to organize a meal for me, once in a while? But Vikram was too frazzled with his kids and his job to respond to my needs. He wasn't interested in commuting between his place and mine. The only way I could enjoy the benefits of his company, was by living with him and his children.

~

The dilemma of my romantic future grew, and so did my dissatisfaction with my existence. My single life was as far removed as possible from what I wanted. I worked all day, and cashed my cheque to support my existence, which I had begun to hate. The apartment was drab, and my child wasn't with me when I needed him to be. Was this what freedom meant?

Every night, I put myself through an inquisition: Is this what you want out of life? To be living alone in a slummy apartment, fending for yourself and putting your kid through the wringer?

Of course, the answer was no. But I didn't know what else to do. The options simply weren't appealing enough: I could move back to my marital home, Vikram's home or my parent's home. Security beckoned in all three, but not nurture. No one said, 'If you come and live here, I will do whatever it takes to make you comfortable and happy.'

Vikram didn't say, let's work out an arrangement that works for you and the children; G didn't say, we'll get a place of our own and start afresh; and my parents didn't say, come and stay, we will accommodate your needs within our house. Nobody promised me a change for the better. All they said was: *Look, we won't change our lives to accommodate you. But you're welcome to join us, if you want. At least you'll be safe.*

The thought of going back to an existence that trapped me in my old self was scary. There was a tiny voice in me, a survival instinct, that said: *None of these choices support your spirit. So wait it out, till you find what does.*

~

My love life was flagging. Vikram and I met less frequently, and when we did, he seemed aloof and distracted. The pressure of being a single parent, combined with his sense of let-down with me, made our time together tense. Soon, I began using my job as an excuse not to go over to his place. By now, I couldn't avoid facing my reluctance to play stepmom, and my lack of maternal feelings was obvious to everyone. Disapproval emanated like a vapour from Vikram's relatives, friends and even his maids and driver. There was no escaping their judgment: women like me, who believe that mothering is a choice rather than female destiny, are considered selfish and deviant.

My stance seemed contradictory to some friends. After all, I was a mother to my own son, who was around the same age as Vikram's children. If I could respond to his needs, why couldn't I do the same for the children of a man I claimed to love? The answer was easy enough for me.

My own decision to have only one child was based on the discomfort I experienced when I had too many people around me. Large families meant clutter and chaos. I found the concept of the modern family, with its multiple members that included exes, their new spouses, stepchildren, and so on, quite terrifying. Having grown used to my only child, I couldn't imagine being part of a new, expanded family.

The only person who refused to confront my true nature was Vikram. He hung on to the illusion that I would come around to accepting his sons and living situation. I should have done both of us a favour by walking away from the relationship the moment I realized our misfit. But how could I? Letting go of love is never easy.

But I was left with no choice. We were eating dinner at Vikram's favourite Italian restaurant, and I was about to bite into the spinach-ricotta ravioli on my plate, when he proposed.

'Let's get married,' he said without any preamble, refilling my glass of Chablis.

I put my fork down, aghast at his suggestion. Why did he have to ruin things?

I took a deep breath, reached out for his hands, and told him it was too soon to get married; that we should give the decision some more thought.

He jerked his hands away, and pushed his plate aside. 'Either you take the leap, or we let it go,' he said flatly, summoning the bill.

I weighed his proposal for two days. The lure of marriage was powerful: becoming Vikram's wife would upgrade my existence in a sweep. I would become a memsahib and live in a big house with numerous maids, stop worrying about ways to earn a living, and resume my short-story writing. Like other women in a privileged position, I could spend hours in a beauty salon getting a mani-pedi and my eyebrows tweezed into shape, and linger over long lunches. Most importantly, being a wife would ensure me the protection and safety that was elusive as long as I was single.

But, the other side of the picture was not so rosy. Wives moved cities and countries every time their husbands' jobs changed, tolerated often-obnoxious in-laws, sacrificed careers and passions for the sake of families and devoted all their energy to responding to others' needs. Everywhere I turned, married women seemed to be bogged down by responsibilities: they were responsible for raising children, managing households, caring for parents, in-laws and extended family members, and managing social situations too.

But the biggest factor that weighed against my marrying Vikram, was my ambivalence about children. Despite my confusion about the direction I wanted my life to take, stepmotherhood was off my agenda. Till this moment, I imagined that love could conquer all. Now here I was, forsaking my relationship with a man who had rocked my universe, based on my decision to live true to my nature.

6

Entering the World of Middle-aged Singles

When my three-year relationship with Vikram ended, I was devastated. Beyond dealing with the sudden absence of a man whose company I enjoyed, I was disillusioned by my own nature. I couldn't avoid facing my distaste for a life that involved taking on the roles most women slid into, almost naturally. If I didn't want to spend my day housekeeping, mothering, and socializing with random people, then what kind of permanent relationship could I possibly anticipate with a man?

Talking to friends and AD eased my fear. My future loomed large and uncertain, but I found some way of convincing myself that my unwillingness to marry Vikram didn't reflect anything other than my current unsure state of mind—a passing phase. Eventually, Mr Right would appear, and I would 'settle down'. The question of how to find him, was another matter altogether.

I grew up at a time when romantic relationships evolved naturally between people who met in school or college, during tuitions, social gatherings or sporting activities. Courtship involved exchanges of handwritten love letters, and eagerly awaited phone calls. Meetings weren't daily affairs, and love stretched over weeks, months and years. Silence and absence fuelled desire. Everyone waited to get married before having sex.

Stepping out single in the Millennium was another matter though. Romance had changed, though I couldn't put my finger on the reasons. So many men and women I knew were addicted to the romantic comedy series, *Sex and the City*, which featured the sexual adventures of four single women in New York. For once, being single was desirable, or so it seemed.

~

In the 60s and 70s, the only women in India who remained single were those who 'failed' to get married. They remained in parental homes, or moved in with brothers or uncles, serving their families till the end of their lives. But by year 2000, every woman faced the prospect of being single at some stage: there was no relying on a standard, predictable life cycle with specific milestones like her mother could. Happily-ever-after love and marriage aren't guaranteed any longer, and the chances of starting a second life in your forties, fifties and sixties have escalated, due to the rise in divorce rates, and increased longevity. Now, women are likely to have at least a couple of serious romantic relationships in their lifetimes.

But, I met many women of my own generation who were uncomfortable with the notion of impermanent love. Although the Western world has embraced middle-age romance in a big way, attributing value to second, third and even fourth romantic unions, Indian society is yet to come around to the idea.

I think that's because lodged somewhere in our heads, is the belief that marriage is for life. Remarriage in late mid-life is more the exception than the norm. Despite all the rhetoric about 'sixty being the new forty', a single Indian women above the age of fifty is regarded as over the hill. Her sexual desires are supposedly sublimated, and all she is expected to anticipate is a future that involves doing social work, or possibly babysitting her grandchildren—if she's been lucky enough to have procreated at some stage.

Though more common, divorce is also still an ugly word for the majority. Indeed, women today are scientists, politicians and historians, and are outspoken, ambitious, won't-stand-for-that individuals in their daily lives, yet they don't transition easily from being married to turning single. I realized this one evening, sitting around a dinner table with a group of middle-aged singles.

The atmosphere was gloomy. Recently divorced women, who identified themselves through their marriages, struggled to find new identities. Being forced to shift from the cozy world of a wife to the floundering universe of singles was traumatic. They hadn't stopped mourning their pasts, and talked as if their lives had been real and meaningful only when they were married.

'Being single at this age feels all wrong,' declared 45-year-old Aditi tearfully. We all nodded understandingly, since she'd experienced the trauma of having her husband walk out on her with her best friend, a plight no woman would wish on another.

Abandonment or bereavement at mid-life is possibly the worst fate imaginable for a married woman. Losing a husband is akin to the loss of a life insurance. Which woman wants to grow old alone, with no one to look after her, or share her life with? Despite the progress made by the women's liberation movement, nothing prepares women for the eventuality of being alone at mid-life.

This was obvious from the stories I heard about the traumatic ending of marriages women had invested years in trying to maintain. That's-how-men-are conversations revolved around cheating husbands and alimony settlements. Feelings of betrayal permeated the room.

'I just couldn't face the fact that my ex-husband was a womanizer and liar from the word go,' declared Aditi. 'I hate myself for waiting till he left me for another woman.' Her statement triggered a debate about whether this was better or worse than being married to a cocaine addict, like 36-year-old Swati. Though Swati was rich from her divorce settlement—which included apartments in South Delhi, London and Turkey—none of this counted because she didn't have a man to keep her company. 'Where *are* all the guys?' she asked plaintively.

Swati had a fulfilling career, opportunities to travel to incredible destinations, eat at Michelin-star restaurants, learn Japanese, macramé or go deep-sea diving. But the focus always returned to the lack of a solid romantic presence in her life which was akin to a gaping hole. She had spent the past two years since her divorce searching for a companion.

Marriage was not her objective, not even a live-in relationship. What she really wanted was a guy she could go to parties, movies and on holidays with. She registered herself on singles' relationship sites, dating apps for older single women, and also called up all her friends—including me—and said: 'Please introduce me to any single guys you know.'

Her courage wasn't dampened by numerous dating mishaps. Once, she set off to see a man she had met online, at a hotel in South Delhi. 'Why don't you have coffee with him first,' we said, when she told us her plans.

Swati shrugged. 'Why bother,' she said. 'May as well just find out what he's like.'

Not surprisingly, the evening was a disaster. The guy was married, and imagined she would be game for a romp. The scenario got ugly when she turned down his sexual overtures, and she was lucky to escape without consequences.

~

Regardless of the circumstances of their lives, the emotional pull of a permanent romantic relationship was strong for everyone. Not a single woman at the table had accepted her aloneness or rather 'husband-less' existence as a possibly permanent condition of her life. Despite fancy degrees, an amazing range of competencies and the capacity to generate good money, there was a finite quality to their feelings about independence.

Even those who had never been married were still waiting expectantly for love to transform their lives. There was 45-year-old Sarika, who lived in her married brother's home and had spent a decade meeting potential suitors lined up by her family. None met her expectations; they were too short, balding, too quick to demand sex, or just too boring. 'The only single guys left for women our age are divorcees with obvious problems, or widowers with children,' she said.

The attention turned to Mamta, another middle-aged single who lived with her parents. At our last meeting, she'd mentioned having met someone new. 'How's it going?' inquired Sarika.

'It's just casual you know,' said Mamta dismissively. 'I mean it's not platonic… but it's not a full-time thing either.'

Her unwillingness to attribute importance to the relationship—just because she couldn't label it—reflected the discomfort many women experienced, about informal or ambiguous romantic relationships. The man-friend may play the unofficial role of husband for many women, but he is still kept under wraps, for fear of judgment. And he will never, ever, provide the sense of permanence or security that a husband does.

Even so, more women were open to unstructured living arrangements with men. When I married in the 80s, live-in relationships in India were seen as the privilege of the rich—politicians, film stars and business tycoons, but not the middle class. This wasn't true twenty years later. Anjali, 48, had invited a man she had been sleeping with a few months, to move in with her.

'He doesn't mind me working while he stays home,' she marvelled.

Most men were threatened by her position as the CEO of a PR company, she said, and this guy was special since he accepted and embraced her success. Really, she loved having an unofficial house-husband. Anjali told us she was supremely grateful to find him waiting for her when she got home from work. 'He's not threatened by me,' she kept saying.

'Why should he be,' snapped Sarika, 'You're giving him a free ride.'

There were some murmurs of discomfort in the room. But Anjali was quick to her own defence. 'Who cares, yaar?'

Her declaration really summed it up for me. Rather than a show of strength, it was an open admission of how desperate she was to have a man, on any terms at all, in her life. Anjali's self-worth hinged more upon the presence of this guy, than the respect she commanded in the workplace, or her expanding bank balance.

~

Finding a romantic partner in mid-life can seem like a lifesaver, a dream come true. In the beginning, there is a sheer sense of relief and joy at having found a man to love. Women float along with their man-friends, too frightened to make demands on them, inevitably falling into patterns without knowing exactly how they were shaped.

Take the case of 54-year-old Suniti, who was thrilled about her new man-friend.

'He's divorced, the CEO of a company, who lives with his daughter and parents,' she boasted, 'a very busy man, a workaholic who thinks holidays are a waste of time.'

When did they conduct their romance then, we quipped curiously. Suniti's face broke into a smile. 'Oh, he manages to slot me into his day.' For her, being 'slotted' into a man's day was better than being alone.

These conversations with my group of women friends made me realize how so many women fall for better-than-nothing relationships, just because they don't want to be alone. Six months ago, Simi, 47, moved in with her man-friend, a divorced man with two teenage daughters and a widowed mother. Despite her successful career in the travel business, a solid group of friends, and a comfortable home of her own, Simi longed to have what she considered a 'normal' life, within a conventional family structure.

The urge to merge overrode the red flags for her. When she moved in with her dream man, things turned sour. She tried to juggle the demands of her job with those at home; arranging for fridge and AC repairs, helping with her man-friend's daughters' school assignments, taking them shopping and for doctors' appointments. In the beginning, she enjoyed being needed.

But then her man-friend turned cold on her. He stopped paying her attention and reimbursing her for household expenses.

'You have a job, don't you, and you're saving what you would have spent living by yourself,' he said, when she brought it up.

Every time Simi suggested they divide the household responsibilities, he made an excuse. 'He says I should be grateful that he's provided me a family home and saved me from being alone,' she lamented to us.

Like Simi, many women hang on to men who aren't any good for them. They tell themselves that since they aren't husbands, they don't owe them anything. Then one day, something happens to expose this lie. They end up heartbroken because of it.

'When my dad died, I called Keshav, crying,' recalls Mita. 'I thought that he'd rush over to comfort me.'

But her long-time lover Keshav didn't show up. Instead, he wrote Mita an email apologizing for his absence—he was travelling and grappling with work deadlines.

Mita was devastated. 'It was as if two people had died instead of one. Here was a man who I had been intimate with, who I imagined cared for me,' she said.

7
Dating Mores According to the Experts

In the West, romantic choices have always been personal, and dictate the decision to marry. When a man and woman are mutually attracted to each other, they date or court, with the intention of getting to know each other. This may or may not lead to a permanent romantic relationship, depending largely on how the man feels. The fate of the relationship is sealed by a guy's willingness to propose, or not. The sad part is that despite the progress made by the women's movement, women still need to work harder than men at persuasion, at every stage of the courtship ritual: first to get guys to fall in love, then to keep their attention and prevent them from straying, and finally, to goad them into making a longterm commitment

Things are different in India. Marriages are less about personal whims, and more about families. Though love marriages are more common today than they were in the 70s and 80s, arranged marriages still dominate. Perhaps that's why romantic love isn't given much importance, and there's a dearth of desi guides to help either women or men navigate their way through the dating maze.

Still, I thought I'd acquaint myself with some dating mores, even if these were Western. Not surprisingly, the majority of popular dating guides are directed at women, who apparently need more help than men, in the department of love. Figuring out what men want is top priority, and there's a plethora of advice and articles of the '7 signs that he's interested in you' type, to help women figure out what a man's behaviour means.

Much is made of 'conflicting' signals of interest. 'If a man takes too long to call you, this could mean either of three things: a. He's just not that interested. b. He's using the delaying tactic to keep his guard up and show that he's in control of the situation. c. He's too busy at the moment.'

Other explanations for confusing signals are equally longwinded and unconvincing. A handful of dating experts advise women to cut through the babble and stop wasting time on men who come up short. The central message of the bestselling guide by Greg Behrendt and Liz Tuccillo, *He's Just Not That into You: The No-Excuses Truth to Understanding Guys,* is: there's not much to speculate about ladies, if a man you fancy doesn't make moves to indicate he reciprocates your interest, then walk away.

The authors slam their views unapologetically into a female reader's face. They say the chances are that a man isn't 'into' you if he doesn't call you; tries to set up meetings with you *only* when he is drunk; refuses to have sex with you but has sex with others; and hasn't proposed marriage. Forget about him and move along, until you find a man who's really into you, ladies.

Women who are too nice are losers, according to another, more provocative and racy book by Sherry Argov: *Why Men Love Bitches: From Doormat to Dreamgirl—A Woman's Guide to Holding Her Own in a Relationship.* Intended for women who are chronically pleasant, the author advises women to lose their niceness and become sharp-tongued 'bitches' instead. She emphasizes that the term 'bitch' is used in a tongue-in-cheek way to describe someone who's 'kind yet strong', an empowered woman who derives 'tremendous strength from the ability to be an independent thinker.'

Some characteristics of a nice girl (that put her in the category of a doormat) are: she sits passively beside her boyfriend while he watches football; cooks him a four-course meal; and drives fifty miles to pick up his dry-cleaning. Stop being such a pushover, commands the author, be a bitch instead. Make a huge fuss, grab the TV remote from your man and put on your favourite show. Never, ever cook for the guy unless it's his birthday. Making some popcorn in the microwave is as far as you should go. Maintaining the upper hand and playing cool will ultimately lead the guy to spin circles around you.

A more low-key approach is recommended by authors Ellen Fein and Sherrie Schneider in their 1995 dating guide *The Rules*, which advocates sitting back and letting the men do the chasing. The authors are adamant that reticence and passivity always win: 'Don't talk to a man first' and 'Don't stare at men' are their commandments. Women can't approach men, call them or make any move whatsoever to indicate they are capable of independent thought.

Women aren't supposed to pay for anything on dates either, since financial independence undermines one's femininity. We must repress our personalities in order to turn into mysterious, alluring sexy sirens that transform men into simpering idiots. Loud, sarcastic, attention-seeking behaviour is absolutely forbidden. Keep your thoughts to yourselves, ladies, allow a man to feel important on all occasions and wait quietly in your bedroom for him to come and get you.

Keeping your legs tightly crossed at all times is also advocated for women who want men to take them seriously, by Kate Taylor's *Not Tonight, Mr Right*. This maintains the moral high ground, advocating complete abstinence from sex and lauding the virtues of chastity. Women aren't made for casual sex, insists the author, since coitus floods the female brain with oxytocin, a neurochemical associated with human attachment. This leads to a suspension of rationality, and tendency to get emotionally entangled with the wrong man. All this business of sexual equality is hogwash! Having the upper hand in a romantic relationship is simply about keeping your panties on, girls.

But things are different for older women. After a certain age, you can't afford to be picky, says Rachel Greenwald, author of *Find a Husband After 35 (Using What I Learned from Harvard Business School)*. Intended to serve as a wake-up call for older single women, this guide recommends that any female above thirty-five come to terms with her limited options. Throw out your want list when it comes to the men, says the author. Unless you make up your minds to choose from the currently available male pool, you are destined to end up on the shelf. So rearrange your lives, ladies, swallow your pride and make a quick pick.

A raunchier dating guide by bad boy Steve Santagati, *The Manual*, promises to educate women on 'How Men Think, Date and Mate'… and what they can do 'to come out on top.' Written by a relationship guru and self-proclaimed 'bad boy', this has a variety of advice for women: how to entice a man, how to dress up to attract, how to maintain the right kind of body, and so on.

A woman's self-esteem is clearly very, very precarious, and the writer says every female must do whatever it takes to build her sense of self. 'Do things for yourself. Buy yourself a gift. Knit a scarf, run a marathon, buy a dog. Anything…' The manual really gets to the nitty-gritty when it comes to grooming advice. Here's one of my favourite tips from the writer: *'Your bikini area is not the place to consider going au naturel. Take care of that area; consider it your Garden of Eden and don't forget to weed it.'*

Apart from good grooming, bubble baths are also mentioned as a path to self-love for women by Cherie Carter-Scott in *If Love Is a Game, Then These Are the Rules*. The book opens with chapter one, on 'How to Love Yourself First'—this advises women to take plenty of bubble baths and watch sunsets. 'With changing roles and soaring divorce rates, men and women today need more help than ever in finding and keeping love in their lives,' says the foreword to this unisex guide to love, which offers diverse tips on a range of concerns, from 'building intimacy to rekindling the faded flame by bringing back the "sizzle factor".'

Another unisex guide intended to turn women into sexual sirens is Robert Greene's *The Art of Seduction*. This 'crash course in how to turn seduction into an art' for both genders advises everyone to get over the idea that love and romance is something magical, and things will simply fall into place. A lackadaisical attitude will get you nowhere, insists the author, since leaving things to chance is a recipe for disaster in love.

Stories of the ploys used by famous men and women to seduce the objects of their interest colour the pages: Helen of Troy, the Chinese siren Hsi Shi, and Cleopatra began by using their appearance to draw men to them, offering tantalizing glimpses of their bodies that served the purpose of inciting the imagination, and ultimately hooking the men. But the women were too smart to give in to the men right away. Instead, they deliberately acted cold and indifferent, confusing them and forcing them into desperate pursuit, and an inevitable decline. Some of the strongest men in history—Mark Antony, Julius Caesar and King Fu Chai were brought down by these women.

A provocative book that makes a big case for men is Steve Harvey's *Act Like a Lady, Think Like a Man*. The author—also a comedian and TV host—wrote this dating guide to help women gain 'insights into the male mind,' many years before he became worldfamous for his blunder of mistakenly announcing the first runner up of the contest as the winner, at the 2015 Miss Universe pageant.

All his advice is sexist, and aimed at getting women to accept, and assume responsibility for, bad behaviour by men. On the subject of cheating, he declares that men cheat because they are weak. But this is a woman's fault: if a man strays, it's because he isn't satisfied in his relationship. Getting a guy to commit is all about 'getting the respect you deserve,' he says, advocating a '90-day Rule,' which prohibits women from having sex with men until the three-month mark. 'Think about it: the first guy you slept with quicker than ninety days—where is he? I'm willing to bet that you're probably not with him,' he says. Regardless of whether your romance blew up in your face because the guy was an alcoholic or a bore, the author says it's always the woman's fault.

Here are Harvey's responses to some 'common' questions apparently asked by women:

> *Q: Will you date or marry a woman who smokes?*
> *A: I wouldn't… the skin of women who smoke ages prematurely. We'll sleep with you but we're not taking you home.*

> *Q: Would a man date a dumb woman?*
> *A: A smart man can't date a dumb woman… we won't mind having a woman on the side who's dumb and fine, but we won't keep her.*

> *Q: How do men feel about women who drink?*
> *A: Remember, men want women to act like ladies all the time…*

Here's my favourite:

> *Q: How do you let a guy know that he's not satisfying you sexually?*
> *A: It's not a good idea to break that news on the kitchen table or on a long car ride. I suggest you break the news while you're in the act. Say something like 'That's nice baby, now do it this way' and watch him go to work.*

8
Conversations Over Coffee

Based on all this collective expert advice on how to snare a man, I realized I needed a new approach, if I expected success. Using feminine strategies of seduction was imperative. I couldn't imagine this, since I've always spoken my mind and expressed my opinions bluntly, traits the dating experts advise against. I argue all the time, and have no idea how to sugarcoat the truth. I laugh loudly and frequently, and hug and kiss people in my circle (including elderly uncles) with abandon.

My parents have a great social spirit, and never discouraged me when I was growing up, so I was shocked when my female gang of advisors told me this habit could easily be misconstrued as 'forward'. 'Don't go around hugging weird guys and laughing too much...they'll think you're into them,' they said. But I enjoyed the light and affectionate banter with men that everyone called flirting, and never considered it a big deal.

In the arena of courtship, however, less was more. Avid female pursuit was strictly forbidden by all relationship gurus, and women had to indicate their interest in men without being obvious. Also, no blurting out of true feelings or needs was permissible. If you really wanted a man, you had to play the female seduction game of hot and cold. Genuine emotions such as attraction or repulsion had no place in the scheme of things.

All these rules seemed ridiculous to me: how was it possible to enjoy an honest relationship with anyone, if games took precedence? It struck me that venturing into such a bleak romantic landscape called for a real leap of faith. If it was so hard for 20- and 30-year-olds to get men to take them seriously, what hope did I—a once married, now single woman of forty, in the city of Delhi—have of stumbling upon a man and relationship that suited my nature and needs?

'Get out there,' said the gang of pals. 'That's the only way to meet new men.'

I came face to face with dozens of middle-aged single women, all of whom seemed to be on a love alert. Many were bolder in their pursuit of a romantic partner than I would have imagined. They didn't wear Manolo Blahnik like *Sex and the City*'s central character Carrie Bradshaw, but they were no less unstoppable. It was as if age had given them the license to shed inhibitions, and simply reach for what they wanted.

Being 'out there' for some meant hanging around bars and clubs, in the hope that they would run into their soulmates. At least a couple of newly divorced women my age were determined to rope me into their find-a-new-man missions. A mate from college, Anita, would squeeze into a little black dress and show up at my doorstep every Saturday night, always with another eager woman in tow.

'Chalo, yaar, we're heading out to this hot little bar in CP,' she'd say, in her most persuasive voice, '…heard the band's really good.'

I always refused: the idea of being perched precariously on a bar stool, trying to chat up men was terrifying and reeked of desperation.

'Don't be such a bore…come with us!' begged Anita, tugging her dress over her bulging hips. 'How do you expect to ever meet anyone?'

'Out there' was an invisible, no-man's land. Discovering it on the South Delhi map was destined to be as frustrating as trying to locate salted caramel ice-cream in a village. My friends egged me on, advising me to stretch my boundaries.

They reminded me that the world was my oyster. That regardless of the dating advice out there, I was free to follow my own head and gut feelings. That I could dispense with the when-to-call and what-to-wear questions, and do my own thing. Women's lib had given me this much freedom, after all.

Yet, I was tentative in the beginning. Meeting a stranger over a cup of coffee seemed bold enough; a relatively safe and inexpensive way of getting a personality snapshot. Though the coffee date has been popular in the West for many decades, we acquired this culture only when Barista and Costa set up cafes at the dawn of the twenty-first century. Before this, freshly brewed coffee could only be had at South Indian restaurants, or five-star hotels.

The Barista experience was far more energizing: the cafes were modern and aromatic from the fresh coffee that hissed out of coffee machines. Sipping a cappuccino or latte between buttery bites of a croissant was a divine experience, which I couldn't get enough of.

'Let's have coffee,' I'd say, to some of the more interesting men I encountered at workplaces, friends' houses, book launches, art exhibitions and parties. They varied in appearance, ages and professions. Some had no hair, and others had too much. There were bachelors, divorcees and even a few widowers. We split the bill, except in one instance when the chap sat back and let me pay, claiming to be a feminist.

I tried to stick to one cup of coffee per meeting (since more than this made me jumpy) and had to curb my instinct to ask probing, interview-style questions: which school did you go to? What does your mother/father/brother do? What's your worst fear? I was careful to avoid bringing up religion, politics and personal philosophy too.

But I did observe the men closely, in an effort to spot characteristics that offered me clues to their personalities. Coffee served as a lens through which I observed them. Google was useful too. Although I had no clearcut relationship agenda, sifting those with romantic potential from the chaff seemed pertinent. Surely our dreams had to match?

All the guys talked about themselves at length, but weren't very interested in hearing what I had to say.

I had cappuccino with a 38-year-old newly divorced guy who spent twenty minutes justifying his decision to surrender custody of his five-year-old daughter to his ex-wife.

'It's all about kismet and karma,' he said, taking a deep breath and looking me straight in the eye, daring me to challenge him. 'My little girl and I will be together in our next life.'

The moment he heard about my interest in health, he told me that he was experimenting with alternative therapies such as Reiki and Ayurvedic shirodhara treatment for his depression. Spiritual pilgrimages were next on the agenda. 'I'm going to Vaishno Devi next week,' he said. I wished him all the best.

I met a man who made a living out of selling toothpaste, and packed as many personal details about himself as humanly possible in our 45-minute meeting: his sleep and meal timings, his favourite cologne, how many times he had travelled to Europe, and the amount of money he had lent—and lost—to cousins and uncles. 'You know I never expected it back,' he said earnestly, leaning towards me. I nearly started clapping.

Then there was a tough, good-looking bodybuilder clad in a muscle-hugging black T-shirt. We had a Rambo-style interaction that involved silences, slurps and a nearly monosyllabic conversation.

I thought about all the discussions I'd had with friends about how sexiness could make up for lack of intellectual compatibility. 'Everyone out there is having sex these days,' said a colleague, quoting the 2005 *India Today* sex survey, which said that urban young singletons 'are shaking off years of conservatism and asserting their sexuality with growing confidence.'

The media was flush with reports about the escalating sales of the morning-after pill, or I-pill, which had apparently become the favoured method of contraception for the urban 'independent' woman. This shocked me. Why would a progressive generation need to maintain the illusion that sex was incidental and accidental? Why weren't women using the daily birth control pill? What about male responsibility, and condoms?

Meeting Mr Muscle confirmed my opinion that sexiness had more to do with the brain, than the body. The few sentences he uttered revolved around his high-protein diet and muscle-building routine. 'You should try it too, Ritu,' he said enthusiastically, reaching out and pinching my arm.

'Ouch!' I uttered, in alarm.

'Too much body fat,' he said dismissively. 'Come to the gym and I'll show you how to get rid of it.'

This casual remark of his triggered a short-lived anxiety attack: was I crazy to be putting myself through this man-meeting exercise? Mid-life was a shocker anyway. Every morning, I woke with new aches and pains, and other random signs of the downward spiral of my body. Lumps of flesh had gathered around my middle. A routine medical checkup revealed high cholesterol and an escalating blood sugar level.

Clearly, my chances of finding romance were doomed unless I cleaned up my act, cut back on the bread and beer, hired a trainer and got a new attitude.

'Jaldi karo, hurry up and find someone...before ultrasounds and X-rays become a regular feature of your life,' jested a brother-in-law, over a dinner of butter chicken and butter naan, accompanied by chilled beer. I took a big swig of my beer in response.

Many of the guys I had coffee with were seriously attached to their phones, and couldn't stop fiddling with them. They scrolled, pushed tabs and sneaked peeks constantly. One got into a loud, ten-minute conversation in Punjabi about a new movie.

'Sorry, overseas call,' he said by way of explanation. A minute later, he picked up my phone and began playing with it. I snatched it back. 'Hey, chill, yaar,' he said, looking put out, as though it was I who had transgressed and not him.

An advertising executive fidgeted with everything he could lay his hands on. He kept moving his cup and saucer around, and rearranging the napkins and spoons on the table. My nerves were fraught by the time he began scratching his head and tapping his foot. My father would probably have asked him why he was so restless and whether he needed to use the toilet.

My coffee dates were an education in the male species, if nothing else!

~

Looking for love must be wildly exciting for young people, but putting yourself out there in your forties and fifties is another thing altogether. It's harder to maintain the illusion that our romantic options are unlimited. Most of us are a little frayed at the edges; bruised by the physical and emotional aftermath of failed relationships and limited in our abilities to develop long-lasting romance and authentic ties with the opposite sex.

'Aren't you too old to be hanging around with men "for fun"?' said the husband of a cousin. He raised his eyebrows when I told him that my intentions were serious; that I hoped to meet someone who could show me a better version of myself. Someone who practiced what he preached and could be counted on at all times. 'You should look for God then,' he retorted sarcastically.

I shrugged and rattled off the list of characteristics I sought in a man: he must be self-reliant, funny, mature and kind; generous and big-hearted; intellectually exciting, with the capacity to discuss philosophy, psychology, and science; active and keen on travel and swimming. My dream guy was the kind to bring home cherries and narcissi when they were in season, put me to bed when I was running on empty, and rub Tiger balm on my temples when they throbbed.

Oh, and he was good-looking as well.

My want list was less ominous than the one I'd had at age twenty, I told myself. At least I wasn't looking for the perfect husband and father any more. I was also more willing to let go of some hang-ups and stereotypes: doctors are lifesavers, weightlifters are strong, and artists are daydreamers.

But at times the stereotypes weren't so off the mark. I sipped mocha with an ageing artist, who went on and on about the grand exhibition he had planned later in the year. He said he needed a personal assistant.

'I want a pretty woman like you to manage my life for me,' he said, winking at me and taking a jab at my arm. He may have been handsome once, but now he was just another lecherous old man.

I thanked him for the offer, and said I already had a job. He appeared taken aback at this rejection: how could any woman—especially one my age—turn down the opportunity to be around him? Like many men of his age, he scoffed at concepts like sexism, feminism and political correctness and acted as if these were a conspiracy hatched against them by the ugly and strident women of the world.

More than one creative man fancied himself to be a reincarnation of Picasso: a very hairy cartoonist boasted about his 'eccentricities' that included drinking a glass of vodka-tonic first thing every morning, and getting a haircut only once every six months.

'Why waste money on a barber, right?'

Mr Hairy lost his last girlfriend after he barred her from coming over for a week. 'I needed space, man...so what if I didn't let her into my place for a few days...I mean, we artists are entitled to a few eccentricities, aren't we?'

Two of my coffee mates were diehard Romeos.

One lived around the corner from me, and was always hanging around the gate when I got home from work.

'Let's have a drink when you're free,' Mr B would say, ignoring the look on my face. It should have been obvious that I had no time or inclination for the proffered drink, but he persisted.

Despite all the hype about the evolution of men and emergence of the 'new age' male, who is sensitive, with the ideal yin-yang balance and so on, the truth was that nothing much had changed.

Indeed, the most popular courtship ritual among men like Mr B was the hunt-and-conquer strategy, based on the behaviour of Bollywood heroes who swaggered about and pursued their heroines ardently, ultimately winning them over. They genuinely believed that no woman would be able to resist them, as long as they were aggressive in their chase.

They made whatever moves they could think of, to indicate romantic interest—stalking their love objects with phone calls, messages and flowers, regardless of the lack of response.

The third time I found Mr B at my gate, I glared at him and said: 'Please go away, I don't want to have a drink with you.' He was very offended at my directness. 'That's too bad for you,' he said as he stalked off and that was the last I saw of him.

Another man kept calling me on the pretext of 'picking my brain' on health matters: *Can you tell me who the best urologist in town is; can you recommend the best tulsi tea in the market; which is the best hospital for a knee replacement for my mum,* and the like. Blocking his number was the only way to stop him.

~

Every few days I told myself to damn rationality; switch off that analytical button in my brain, and be reckless with someone unsuitable—like a polo player or a film star. But the only actor I met was stringy-haired and unshaven, and sported a jhola: he hadn't got beyond the waiter or villain role in movies. He supported himself by conducting 'stress-busting' workshops, which I'd reported on in one of the Sunday papers.

Our coffee session was a disaster. It started badly, since he arrived twenty-five minutes late.

'Sorry, yaar, shooting went on longer than expected... you know I'm in a new film right?' Sweat trickled down his neck and he looked more unkempt than before.

I recoiled, and told him I had to leave soon.

'But I wanted to talk about your article... How come you left out my major movie roles?' he said, sounding peeved. 'Can you do one of those errata thingies?'

Thankfully for him, my cup of coffee arrived scalding hot and my tongue was too burned for me to tell him that he should be grateful I wrote anything about him at all—he had never had a major role in any film.

Most of my coffee dates were poor company, since they were incapable of a real conversation. They started out by asking me questions, but ended up talking about themselves. Some guys were hung up on one thing, and talked about it incessantly: the insomniac about his sleepless nights, the cycling maniac about how fantastic it was to wake at 4 a.m. daily to do his 20-km ride, and the emotionally injured businessman who couldn't recover from the fact that he had to pay a lakh a month as maintenance to an ex-wife who earned more than he did.

'Talk about rights! Women get away with such bullshit in the name of feminism,' he said angrily, thumping the table.

I tried to look sympathetic though I was more worried about my cappuccino, which had sloshed all over my saucer. He rushed to get some napkins and mop up.

His was the first tale of many about mean exes and scheming in-laws. I realized that men's accounts of breakups could be as dramatic as those of women. Listening to them rambling on about their woes was strangely pleasing on occasion: it made me feel sane, so very rational and down to earth.

My coffee encounters excavated my deep-seated contempt of men I hadn't realized till then that I had. It shocked me that no one ever measured up to my expectations. No male was strong enough, clever enough, smart enough or idealistic enough. Everyone I met either seemed to have commitment issues, was gay, or a serial dater, wimpy, boorish or utterly incapable of a healthy adult relationship with any woman. I began thinking that most Indian men who weren't hitched by their forties were better off alone.

I drank hazelnut-flavoured latte on two occasions with a tall, blue-eyed American CEO of a development agency working to provide safe water and sanitation to rural India. He'd made some moves on me during a seminar on rural sanitation, claiming to be impressed with my science writing. I was flattered, until I realized that he was keener on educating me on issues of development, than romancing me.

At our first meeting, he droned on about drinking-water issues: *India was the worst-off country in the world, when it came to safe drinking water...Water tables were falling and water sources were shrinking...*

The solution, he lectured, was for communities to take over the management of rural water supply schemes: I should write about it, he said.

I nodded dully, sipping the fragrant brew, and swallowing my disappointment at the false romantic promise of his blue eyes.

I was even stupid enough to agree to a second meeting, which gave him a chance to lecture me about sanitation problems, specifically, the dangers of human excreta.

'Did you know that fifty kinds of infections can be transmitted from diseased people to healthy ones, through shit?'

My coffee suddenly looked browner and murkier. It struck me that those committed to a cause could be dreadfully boring, especially if one didn't share their passion. And that discussing shit while you are drinking coffee is highly offensive.

Like my blue-eyed American, so many men I met made off-colour remarks during mealtimes, or bombarded me with the kind of personal revelations that should never, ever emerge during a meal. Once, I sat across the table from a picky eater who told me about his numerous gastrointestinal ailments: how broccoli gave him gas and the vinegar in salad dressing caused acid reflux.

Then there was a meal with a guy who kept digging his chicken leg with a spoon.

'My mum died when I was just ten, so I never learned how to use a fork and knife… my stepmother left me to eat with the servants, in the kitchen,' he said by way of explanation when he caught me staring at him.

I sympathized, but couldn't bring myself to either teach him to use cutlery, or have another meal with him.

Guys who wouldn't stop drinking during a meal were another kind of meal dampener. They became more and more garrulous as the evening progressed, ruining my appetite and diminishing my eating pleasure. And then there were smokers, who wouldn't stub out their cigarettes. 'Sorry about this,' one said, indicating his cigarette, 'but it serves as a substitute for sex.'

Loud, rude men made the worst companions of all. One chap I had dinner with was enraged at the amount of garlic in his chicken. He banged the cutlery and summoned the waiter.

'Get the chef here for me,' he yelled. This was just the beginning. 'Are your tastebuds dead or what?' he said, picking up his plate and shoving it in the face of a frightened staffer, wearing a chef's hat.

It took all evening and a complimentary meal to appease him. People at the tables around us kept throwing disgusted looks at me, and I wanted to hide my face in my handbag.

~

My longest and final coffee meeting was with N, a cousin's brother-in-law, a scientist of some sort whom I'd met several years earlier, during my married days. He lived in London, and I recalled him as a verbose somewhat eccentric man, who always donned black Levis and collared shirts, regardless of the season. When he suddenly appeared on the scene and asked me out, I was taken aback.

My memory of him was kinder than reality. N had a bald spot on his crown and stooped a bit. But he seemed delighted to see me. 'Ritu, Ritu…it's been too long.' He tried to hug me in a full frontal kind of way, but I managed to wedge my handbag between us. Still, this didn't diminish his elation at meeting me.

'You have no idea how much I've thought about you,' he declared.

Should I be flattered, I wondered. The last time I'd heard this line was from a man in my social circle whom I'd barely noticed. Funny how the men totally off my radar seemed more interested in me, than those I was attracted to.

N summoned the waiter and ordered a selection of cakes and tarts with our coffee.

'You always liked strawberry tart, didn't you?' he said, in the fond manner of a long-time friend. I was flummoxed—how did he know this? I couldn't remember having interacted with him long enough to share my food preferences.

'Oh, thanks,' I muttered, feeling foolish.

He launched into a description of the joys of strawberry-picking, one of his favourite summer pastimes. 'The English countryside is spectacular, as you probably know.'

I nodded nostalgically, recalling the rolling greens, scones with clotted cream and beer on tap that made my last trip there memorable. 'Travel in Britain is so easy,' I mused, 'you can get from one end to another so quickly…it's so small.'

He started to tell me about his recent trip to Hanoi. 'Did you know that Vietnam has some really talented artists?' he said, pulling out his phone to show me photos of two paintings he'd just bought. 'Do you travel much, Ritu?'

I shrugged. 'A few times a year, usually on work,' I said.

'It must be nice to get out of Delhi, it's such a hellhole,' he said conversationally, spearing a strawberry out of his tart with great finesse, 'especially for women who live alone.'

'Don't you live by yourself too?' I countered, irritated. Why did Indian men who lived abroad always seem more regressive than their brothers in desi villages?

He shrugged and raised his eyebrows. 'Sure, but I'm a single male in London, not a single woman in Delhi,' he said, leaning towards me. 'But then I'm sure your life must be far more exciting than mine.'

I frowned. 'Why is that?'

He gave me a sly, sideways look. 'Oh come on…life in the single lane for an Indian woman your age is bound to be exciting.'

The insinuation was obvious, and I fought my impulse

to hit him. Instead, I summoned the waiter and ordered another tart for myself. *May as well let him pay for his presumptuousness.*

'Want some more?' I said nonchalantly, gobbling the tart as if it was about to run away. He looked disgusted. 'No thanks, I'm full.'

'So how's your work these days?' I said, keeping my tone flippant. 'You work in one of those labs, right?'

He looked affronted. 'Actually I am a senior research scientist, and my work involves the development of cutting-edge drugs,' he said testily.

For the next five minutes, he described the new drug his company had developed for Alzheimers. I summoned the waiter and asked for more coffee. N looked annoyed at my interruption. I ignored him and began fidgeting with my napkin.

'Anyway, I wanted to tell you about my holiday plans for summer,' he continued, looking at me in that 'You're never going to know what I did last summer' way.

I looked beyond him, through the windows, at the bottlebrush tree that was in full bloom, and tried to guess what kind of vacation someone like him would enjoy. Certainly not sky diving, snorkelling or lying around on a beach… I couldn't imagine him in swimming trunks…

'So where are you off to?' I inquired dutifully.

'The Bahamas,' he stated dramatically, his eyes holding mine. I looked away and shook my head in disbelief.

'Why don't you come with me?' he asked, maintaining a deliberately casual tone and reaching for my hand across the table. 'All expenses paid of course.'

I jerked my hand away and curled it into a fist, overcome again by the urge to smack him.

9

Married and on the Make

Though entertaining enough, my coffee adventures didn't uplift my life in any tangible way. Most mornings I woke with a sense of dismay; my dark, stuffy apartment with its garlic-tinged air induced a feeling of nausea. The thought of having to maintain the daily banter with my neighbours, and continue to fend off the landlady's attempts to intrude into my life, was overwhelming.

My job selling books had met with a natural death when I started locking myself up in the office bathroom, to avoid making the daily sales calls. The number of people joining the BK network dwindled. My days at BK Books were numbered, and my enthusiasm for my newfound 'independent' lifestyle waned correspondingly.

I was sick of making trips to the Delhi Jal Board and BSES office to sort out escalated water and electricity bills. I was fed up of being ripped off by workers who treated women like me as retards: the electrician who forced me to pay Rs 1000 for a condenser he hadn't used; and the plumber who insisted upon changing the whole flushing system of my toilet, when all that needed replacing was a valve.

Some part of me was simply waiting for a man to step in and take over my life. The only reason I had got so far, was because I had imagined my new lifestyle was temporary, a stopgap arrangement till I got together with

Vikram. Like so many other women, the subconscious lure of marriage as the ultimate life-changer remained powerful. The ending of my relationship with him rendered me directionless.

We are geared for dependency, instead of freedom, and are surprised when we find ourselves alone by accident. We tell ourselves that it's just for now, and that our Prince Charming is out there somewhere, it's just a matter of time before he makes his appearance. Some women I've met live makeshift lives, since they live in anticipation. They eat scrappy meals, as 'there's no point in organizing a meal, just for myself.' Why bother, they say. Others keep perfect homes, but neglect their grooming. 'Who cares about those extra kilos, or getting that haircut… there's no one to please.' It's as if we can't grant ourselves permission to live well, eat well, spend money on ourselves, look good, be happy, and feel complete in our lives—unless there's a man somewhere in the picture.

I walked on the broken sidewalks of the city, sidestepping dog shit and wondering where my dreams of self-discovery and romance had evaporated. All I could see was the peeling wall in my bedroom, the broken kitchen cupboard and the acid caking the terminals of the inverter. How to summon up the energy and resources to fix all of this?

Where was my knight in shining armour?

∼

My angst reduced after I successfully negotiated a lease for a lovely second-floor flat in a greener, quieter part of the city. Through my new windows, I looked out at treetops. My two-roomed apartment in Chittaranjan Park was bright and airy, since it faced a park. I woke to birdsong and the calls of vendors who began their rounds at daybreak—vegetable sellers, mochis, jharu-walas, and nali-walas—specialists in removing fishbones from blocked drains!

I settled down quickly this time: the practical aspects of setting up home were less overwhelming, and the welcoming attitude of the landlord, Mr Chakraborty, and his wife, eased the transition. My living conditions were remarkably better; power cuts were rare in the area, and water gushed out of the taps. The market around the corner was lush with fresh vegetables, fruit and fish. I developed a taste for rose-flavoured kancha gollas from Annapurna and the egg rolls sold by roadside vendors.

Good food resumed its place in my life after I found a part-time cook, Arti, who churned out sumptuous Bengali fare—fish curry, paneer posto, luchis, kheer and all kinds of spinach preparations. Over the next few months, my despondency abated, and I felt ready for new challenges.

～

On a whim, I responded to an advert for an editor at a bridal magazine, and actually landed the job. Friends and family were aghast at the thought of my taking on the 'frivolous' work of pondering over wedding decorations and honeymoon travel packages. Surely I should put my education to better use? But I was excited nonetheless at the prospect of working for a glossy women's magazine, so radically different from the science pages of the papers I usually wrote for.

Bridal Matters was run out of a one-room office located

on the barsati floor of a house in Golf Links, above the publisher's apartment. A whole wall was covered with quotes about love and marriage. My favourite was: *Marriages are made in heaven. Divorces on earth. Don't take chances.* I liked the dramatic sound of this gibberish, though I had no idea what it meant.

'Marriage is a gift that shouldn't be squandered,' explained Luke Adams, the 55-year-old publisher of *Bridal Matters*. I bit back a sarcastic retort, and settled my face into an agreeable expression. There was no point in launching into my negative view of marriage, especially since I had chosen to earn a living through a publication devoted to supporting the institution. I wondered how long my attempt at political correctness would last.

Though Luke was born in Goa, he had immigrated to the UK during his youth. He was in Delhi for a couple of years with his wife Sandra, a highflying advertising executive whose company had posted her in the city. The idea of a wedding magazine arose when Luke realized that the big fat Indian wedding could be capitalized upon. 'Why not milk it, right, love?' he asked me at our first meeting

Until I arrived, Luke functioned as the editor of the magazine with the help of three young women: a stylist, a writer and a PR executive. Though they looked like fresh college graduates, the trio was bright and enthusiastic. They welcomed my company in the office, and brought me cups of masala chai every few hours to perk me up.

Editing a low-budget monthly wedding magazine was an almost surreal experience. Every month, I had to plan a 100-page issue of articles and photos centered on wedding trivia: how to plan your wedding right; how to prepare your trousseau; the right makeup and hairstyles for the big day; dry flower arrangements; gifting ideas for men and women; honeymoon destinations, and so on.

I was forced into the role of writing copy too, since we couldn't afford to pay writers who could write well enough. Make-believe honeymoons became my specialty: I spent hours summoning up adjectives to describe a cruise down the Nile, or the view of Paris from the top of the Eiffel Tower. *Bridal Matters* also carried stories on newlywed couples, and featured celebrity weddings. Fortunately the trio in the office took turns attending these with the photographer, and I simply churned out captions and splashy headlines. It was a relief to do the kind of work that didn't involve the degree of social interaction my job at BK Books had called for.

There was an Agony Aunt kind of advice column, *Ask Asha,* which was very popular with the readers. Dozens of young newlywed women wrote in with their problems: how to keep in-laws from interfering with their relationship, 'my money-your money matters,' and more sensitive 'between the sheets' kind of issues.

A highbrow counsellor called Asha had been the original Agony Aunt, till Luke dismissed her. 'She didn't respond to half the letters, saying the problems were too trivial for her to pay attention to,' he complained. By the time I joined, Asha had been replaced by the kindly Dina, who mulled carefully over every dilemma, and came up with solutions that didn't rock the Indian family boat.

If there was a complaint about a mother-in-law, for instance, her advice would be the 'try and look at things from her point of view' kind. So when Dina announced that she was moving to Chennai as her husband had been transferred there, Luke was delirious with worry. 'Look for someone to take over, fast,' he said, rushing out of the door.

An hour later, he was back in the office with a huge box of fudge brownies. 'To celebrate the appointment of our new Agony Aunt—Ritu Bhatia,' he said, opening the box with a flourish and handing it around to everyone. Before I could open my mouth to protest, Luke said, 'Oh come on—you don't need a degree in psychology to advise people.'

My new role as marriage counsellor added another dimension to my job. I took this very seriously indeed: It was a chance to change women's lives for the better, to get them to stand up for themselves and create marital relationships that met their needs. I wanted to contribute actively to the social revolution that seemed to be in motion, which was prompting women to evaluate men and relationships more closely.

So, when a letter arrived, I went to great lengths to discuss the problem posed in it with my colleagues, as well as my personal advisory group, before shooting off a response. Despite Luke's instruction to offer 'balanced' advice, I usually ended up suggesting solutions that liberated women from what was domestic bondage, in my head.

Rather than recommending accommodation and adjustment to husbands and in-laws, I went on a rampage advising the ladies to live on their own terms: it was time women learned that self-preservation was more important to their happiness than being a good-natured pushover.

Here are some letters, with my responses:

Q: Dear Asha: I've been married for two years, and my husband is pressurizing me to get pregnant. But I love my job, and feel that a baby will only get in the way. What to do? Pls help!—Ms Libertina
A: Dear Ms Libertina: Follow your heart. If you aren't ready to have a baby, say it out loud, to anyone who will listen. If your husband won't hear no, just start taking the pill. You won't be the first woman to do this.

Q: Dear Asha: My mother-in-law insists that I wear only Indian clothes. But giving up my jeans and switching to salwar kameez and sarees is like a punishment for me. What to do?—Ms Distressed
A: Dear Ms Distressed: Life is too short to spend in Indian clothes. Give your salwar kameezes to the maid, and get back into your favourite pair of jeans. Your husband can give his mother the good news, and perhaps even take her shopping for a pair of her own.

While Luke admired my forthright nature, he didn't take kindly to what he considered 'tactless' and 'radical' suggestions. Things came to a head when I advised a middle-aged woman whose husband was having an affair, to dump him.

'*Dear Mrs Betrayed,*' I wrote, '*once a man's cheated on you, he's going to do it again and again, so get up and walk away.*'

Instead of applauding my no-nonsense stance, Luke said my attitude was preposterous and unreasonable. He soon found an elderly counsellor to take over the column.

I didn't protest, since I was bored with my advisory role by now.

Coincidentally, one of my ex-collegemates, Neena, came home for dinner around this time. We were meeting after a decade, and she didn't try to hide how thrilled she was that I'd joined the singles club. She had plenty to say about how men regarded women 'like us'.

'All sorts of guys will hit on you, all the time,' Neena declared dramatically. 'So prepare yourself.'

I was startled at her bleak view of men. 'Don't be silly,' I retorted. 'Why would they do that?' She let out an exasperated sigh. 'Because they believe you are available,' she said wryly. 'The married guys are the worst,' she continued. 'But don't ever make the mistake of getting involved with someone else's husband.'

Her warning didn't strike me as relevant, since I wasn't worried about the pitfalls of getting involved with married men. The only married guys I encountered were friends' husbands, and colleagues. The chances of my striking up an affair with any of these guys were remote. I couldn't imagine becoming the 'other woman' anyway: retreating to the sidelines of a man's life, pining for him to leave his wife and ultimately ending up a psycho, like Glen Close in *Fatal Attraction*.

But Neena had been the 'other woman', and felt bound to warn her friends against making the same mistake. She had spent four years in a relationship with a married businessman, who struggled to cater to the demands of his wife, teenage daughter and ageing parents. Though she came last, Neena didn't care in the beginning. 'Meeting whenever we could was good enough,' she says.

Her flat served as their love shack, and they went on short trips together once in a while, at Neena's expense. 'I paid for tickets and hotels, since he couldn't account for these expenses at home,' she explained. It never struck her how easy she made life for her married lover; or that her accommodating attitude only served to fuel his duplicity.

When her worried friends cautioned her against keeping the relationship going, she'd get angry with them: *What do you expect me to do when you know there aren't any single men of my age around… He loves me much more than he loves her, it's just a matter of time… He's better than all the guys I've been with so far…*

One year of togetherness turned into three, and nothing changed. Her lover made no move to change the status quo, and Neena accepted the inevitable. 'I'm only ever going to be the other woman,' she said bitterly. Every time she asked him when he planned to divorce his wife, he would say, 'Please give me some time; let my kids grow up a little.' Then it became 'I'll leave my marriage once the children get married.'

Neena knew deep down that he wouldn't get a divorce. Even if a marital relationship is a living hell, most Indian men will hang in there for the sake of their children, parents, aunts, uncles, in-laws and the rest of the world. That's what a 'Made in India' marriage is all about. A man willing to walk away from his commitment is rare. And even if he does choose love over duty, the consequences of his decision on the 'other woman' are often heartwrenching, since she has to work doubly hard to make his 'sacrifice' worthwhile.

~

Occasionally I enjoyed playing the 'what if' game: what if I'd married my first boyfriend when he proposed; what if I'd studied English literature instead of microbiology; what if I'd taken up my father's offer to do a PhD abroad; what if I'd said yes to the invitation I'd received from one of my professors, to work in Boston? Daydreaming about how different my life could have been was a pleasurable pastime. Every time I met someone from school or college, I lapsed into this mode.

I was at the dentist's when I ran into an ex-collegemate, Rajan. Twenty-five years earlier, we'd competed in debates organized by the university—we were the captains of debating teams from our respective departments. We sparred verbally on many issues: 'Greening our planet', 'Civic Responsibility,' 'Consumer Rights' and so on. Though his hair was slick with oil and he wore a jacket even in the summer, Rajan was full of bright ideas, and we got on well.

On occasion, I would be ribbed about this by a collegemate. 'Kuch kuch ho raha hai…something's up between you two, isn't it?' I shook my head in annoyance. The thought of being paired with him was scary. Rajan was just too tradition-bound; a rule-abiding Indian male who lived life based on family and societal expectations.

His life was one long plan, which began when he finished school: there was the MBA, followed by a prized job in a multinational company, marriage to a fair and demure woman chosen by his parents, and all the other markers of success. I, on the other hand, prided myself at that time, on having defeated the female stereotype. I was studying for an MSc degree, drove a car, was in the college swimming and debating teams and had never made my own bed or cooked a meal. In fact; I was the antithesis of the kind of woman who would settle down with Rajan.

Over two decades had elapsed since our last meeting. Rajan sported a potbelly, and a receding hairline. But the red string or mauli around his wrist and the gemstones glowing on his fingers marked him as my college pal. Despite the rational arguments he presented during our debates, Rajan had never been able to escape his own superstitious nature. He wore rings of sapphires and rubies, stones that supposedly protected him from the evil spirits. He made a visit to the temple every single day, saying that he couldn't function minus God's blessings. He wore his mauli till it dissolved in his own sweat.

Rajan looked up from the magazine he was reading. His eyes lit up with recognition.

'Aren't you Ritu Singh from Panjab University?' he asked.

'Yes, I am, Rajan!' I responded, elated at meeting someone from bygone days. We laughed and exchanged phone numbers.

He called the next day, and we chatted for a while. Rajan told me he'd made a career as a financial consultant, and spent the last decade working in Argentina. He'd invested well, achieved his mission of providing his daughter a Western education. Now, he was back in India. 'It's time for a new chapter in life,' he announced earnestly, 'though I can afford to retire if I feel like.'

The conversation turned to me. He asked what I'd been up to. What did my husband do? I told him about my career as a journalist and my current job as the editor of a bridal magazine.

'I have a teenage son and live in CR Park,' I said, trying to be vague about my personal life.

Rajan wasn't having it though. 'So why did your marriage break up?' he prodded.

I sighed. What was I to say? That I didn't try hard enough? That my husband and I had mismatched personalities? The age difference was too much? Whatever reasons I cited wouldn't be good enough: desi women don't have the luxury of ending marriages unless they are beaten by their husbands or hounded for dowry by their in-laws.

Rajan's voice butted into my thoughts. 'I never imagined that a woman as beautiful as you would end up alone,' he said.

'Oh, you don't have to worry Rajan... I've never been alone in my life,' I snapped, annoyed at this complacent married man using the 'poor you' card on me. Rajan was quick to cover up.

'Oh, I'm sure... someone like you will always have a line of admirers,' he said glibly.

I relaxed, smiling at the deft manner in which he had manoeuvered the conversation. A wave of nostalgia overtook me, as I recalled our long, animated conversations in the canteen, over samosas and tea. So when he suggested a coffee, I agreed immediately. What could possibly be wrong with meeting up with an old friend from college, a happily married guy who posed absolutely no threat whatsoever?

We met at Barista, around the corner from my home. Rajan greeted me effusively, standing up to give me a half hug. I was taken aback, since I didn't remember him being the hugging kind. Still, I managed to keep my smile on.

He ordered a cold coffee with ice cream, and an Americano for me. We chatted about the goings-on of collegemates. He told me about his master plan for life, which extended over the next two decades: career moves, insurance matters, investments, retirement plans, and the like. No aspect had been ignored, and there was no space for anything new and unexpected, either. My own existence seemed so precarious in comparison.

'You'll be pleased to know that my daughter Tina is following in your footsteps—she wants to be a journalist,' he said, looking intently at me.

I took a bite of biscotti and raised my eyebrows. 'That's great,' I said, trying to hide my surprise that he'd turned out to be a progressive father after all. So much for my feeling that the only place Rajan believed women should rule was the kitchen.

'She's in Wellesley,' he said, proudly, leaning forward to see my reaction.

I tried to look suitably impressed but I felt curiously despondent at the idea that Rajan's daughter was in one of the most famous women's liberal arts colleges in the world. So many eminent women, including the writer Nora Ephron and politician Madeleine Albright, were ex-alumni.

I stared at the red string around his wrist, and fiddled pensively with my own silver bracelet. Success and failure were so fragile. Just last year, I had signed a contract with a big publisher for a collection of short stories. But I was making absolutely no progress on the book. I lacked the drive and discipline it took to write every day. Would things have turned out differently if I'd taken a course in creative writing, instead of studying microbiology?

Rajan's voice broke me out of my reverie. 'It was Tina's own idea—her mother and I had nothing to do with her admission there,' he admitted. 'She got a partial fellowship to pursue media studies.'

I wondered what Rajan's wife was like. Was theirs a happy marriage? It was hard to tell from his manner and conversation.

~

A month went by before I heard from Rajan again.

'Hi—I'm in your neighbourhood,' he said breezily, on the phone. 'Can I drop in?'

From his tone, it was obvious he wasn't asking for permission.

Five minutes later, he was at my front door, panting from the exertion of climbing two flights of stairs. 'For you,' he said, handing me a gigantic bunch of red roses with a flourish.

I thanked him, sniffing the heady perfume, and wondered if I had a vase big enough for the flowers. Rajan strolled in and made himself at home right away. He wandered around my drawing room, picking up objects and examining the paintings on the wall.

'Lovely place, Ritu...but then you always had good taste,' he said, softly.

He bent down to get a closer look at the pattern of my Afghan dhurrie and upturned a blue ceramic vase to identify the maker. 'Made by a potter friend of mine,' I said.

Rajan put it down and settled himself into my favourite armchair. 'Hmm, nice,' he murmured.

I followed him around, restlessly settling cushions and readjusting the wall hangings, feeling uneasy at the familiarity of Rajan's manner.

I recalled my friend Neena's advice about keeping married men at a distance. Maybe I should have made some excuse to keep him away. Then I told myself I was reading too much into it. Rajan was just a mate from university days, and I was simply being friendly.

'What will you drink?' I asked, struggling to recall if he was a teetotaler or not.

Rajan responded immediately, as if he had been waiting for this question. 'Whisky and soda, if you have some,' he said, looking around the room to see if he could spot a bottle somewhere.

His transparency was touching. I took out a bottle of Black Label from the kitchen cupboard and poured him a drink, topping it up with soda and ice.

He had a big gulp, emptying half the glass in one go. 'Aren't you drinking anything?' he said, suddenly realizing that I was empty-handed.

'Don't worry, Rajan, I'll get myself something,' I said, pulling out a bottle of Kingfisher from the fridge.

I handed him a bowlful of chips and carried another one for myself to the sofa. Rajan swished his drink around, knocking the ice cubes together before taking a sip.

'So Ritu, what's it like being a single woman?' he asked

I shrugged, feeling a trifle annoyed at the way he said 'single'. It rankled, because it implied a special status, a condition even, rather than a normal state of being.

Someone needed to invent a new label, I decided. 'It's different from being married, Rajan,' I said coldly.

Rajan was perched at the edge of the sofa, nodding. 'And?'

'I never thought I would enjoy living alone,' I added, shaking my head in wonder.

He snorted in disbelief, and stood up. 'I need a refill, please.' I poured him another drink, and we sat and munched our chips companionably.

'What about you, Rajan—what's family life been like for you?' A shadow crossed Rajan's face and he took a deep breath before launching into his story. 'Ritu, you know I met my wife Tulsi through the matrimonials,' he began. 'My parents and I chose her together.'

There was no reason not to: Tulsi was good-looking, a devout Hindu, and potentially an ideal wife and mother. Things were good in the beginning.

'She was moody, but I didn't pay much attention to this,' he recalled. They had one child, their daughter Tina, and when she turned ten, Rajan had the opportunity to move to Argentina.

'It was a big break,' he said. 'A chance to make enough money to last us a lifetime.'

But a year after the move, Tulsi became depressed and listless. She lost interest in everything. She wouldn't get out of bed for days at a stretch, didn't pay any attention to their daughter, wouldn't get dressed, and stopped taking care of the house.

'She was diagnosed with manic depressive syndrome,' Rajan said despondently. After this diagnosis, things went downhill. Despite medication, his wife was dysfunctional for long stretches, compelling Rajan to send Tina to a boarding school.

'I managed to get her into Sanawar for a couple of years before she left for college,' he said.

Rajan's tale was moving. I could only imagine how tough it must have been for a man like him, who had been raised to expect a conventional life—a good wife, a couple of children, probably some grandchildren. Being handed the mental illness card was no small matter.

'Must have been tough on you,' I sympathized.

'I couldn't believe my bad luck,' he admitted. 'But then my guru said it was written in my horoscope and I simply had to find a way to be happy, regardless. So I grabbed the chance for a new life the moment it arose.'

The tension in Rajan's voice broke for an instant, and I could feel my exasperation rising, like it had in the past when Rajan's conversations had turned to spiritual matters. Clearly, his habit of relying on godmen, astrologers and face readers to help him make his decisions, hadn't disappeared.

'I fell in love with an Argentinian colleague, Teresa,' he confessed. What started out as an affair to distract him from his unhappy home life, ended up changing his life. Rajan lost interest in his wife and started envisioning a new future with his lover.

'But didn't you feel bad about cheating on your wife, especially since she was disabled in a way?' I blurted out.

Rajan was unperturbed. 'Not really,' he said. 'My marriage was a sham.'

Unfortunately for him, his relationship with Teresa didn't work out, as his decision to get a divorce from his wife came to nought.

'Believe it or not, it was Teresa who stopped me. She said she wouldn't dream of breaking up my marriage... that my wife needed me more than she did,' he said sorrowfully.

I stared, dumbstruck, at him, struggling to reconcile my image of Rajan from college, with this newer, updated version—a man who had actually considered abandoning his wife and settling down with an Argentinian woman. Clearly, I had underestimated him.

'So what did you do?' I said, refilling his glass and trying to contain my impatience to know how things had turned out.

'Nothing. What could I do? I packed up and came back to India,' he said. 'Teresa left me no choice in the matter.'

I lapsed into a thoughtful silence, unsure of how to react to Rajan's confessions. They felt too personal. I was uncomfortable at being drawn into the lives of so many people I had never met. But I told myself it didn't matter; that his ready sharing of intimate information reflected the natural evolution of our friendship.

He was a different man today, not the conservative collegemate of the past, I thought, a conclusion that was shaken by his next declaration.

'If it hadn't been for my guruji, I wouldn't be alive today,' he said emotionally.

Based on his guru's advice, Rajan fed moong dal and basmati rice to the cows, and threw numerous metallic objects into the Ganges for six months after his return to India. Miraculously, his domestic situation improved, and his angst over his shattered love life disappeared.

'My mother-in-law lives with us now, and looks after

everything at home,' he said happily. 'I am free to do whatever I like.' He gave me a meaningful look and I knew my misgivings had been right.

I'd heard enough. I stood up and started clearing the glasses. It was time for my evening TV show, *Grey's Anatomy*, my daily fix of fantasy. I wanted to be alone with the lusty physicians on my screen, to curl up on my couch with a cheese toast. Today I would know whether the lead character, the whimsical Dr Meredith Grey, would marry the sexy neurosurgeon Derek.

I started banging the cupboards in the sitting room open and shut, as though I was looking for something, in my impatience to get rid of Rajan. Time to go home, man! He, though, took this as a cue to open the cupboard closest to him. 'Is this where you keep the whisky?' he said.

I snatched the bottle from him. 'Thanks, I'll put it away.'

⁓

I didn't see Rajan for another month, though he called every week to give me a bulletin on his life; the trips he made for work, his daughter Tina's progress, and so on. I wasn't really interested, but felt some strange sense of obligation to listen anyway. I volunteered some random information on myself, chosen to amuse rather than anything else.

Since he was so caught up in himself, the opportunity to discuss anything relevant in my own life didn't arise anyway. One morning, we met accidentally at the Dera farms shop.

'Are those any good?' he inquired, when I asked for some Parsi kebabs.

He suggested I try some pre-cooked Thai chicken. 'Tina is in town you know... and she just loves it,' he said.

'Then I must get some,' I said, amicably.

'Why don't you come for dinner and meet her... and my mother-in-law and wife, of course,' he said.

Though I told myself his invitation to meet the family was just a friendly gesture, I've never really understood why married people aren't sanctioned to pursue independent friendships with members of the opposite sex. Establishing a fake camaraderie with the husband or wife of an ex-flame appears to be the only socially acceptable way to keep up the connection. *How tiring.* I recalled my reunion with my first boyfriend after thirty years, which took place under his wife's supervision. I can still recall my disappointment at his lack of courage. Why couldn't he have taken me to lunch alone?

'Thanks Rajan, but I have some people coming over tonight,' I said, collecting my packages and moving towards my car.

His face fell, but he recovered his composure quickly. 'Sure, talk soon then.'

And then Rajan just disappeared. I wondered about him off and on, but wasn't compelled to call him. He was just another casual friend, a married man, and not someone I was attracted to. An occasional connection with him was good enough for me.

So when he dropped out of sight, I assumed it was because he was busy—travelling, or bogged down by his job, or family obligations. Since it was my instinct to switch to passive mode whenever I felt uncertain about the nature of a relationship, I felt relieved at his absence.

My job at *Bridal Matters* compensated for the excitement missing in my personal life. Luke decided the team would accept an offer made by the Sri Lanka tourism department, to fly us there and put us up in the best resorts. We would arrange a series of fashion shoots, one in each location. I was put in charge of the project.

'You need to get a team together quickly, Ritu,' he ordered.

The office was thrown into a frenzy: there were outfits and accessories to be chosen for the shoots, travel itineraries to be planned and collaborations to be set up with designers in Sri Lanka. The trip was spectacular though. The magazine team, along with models, photographers and fashion stylists, spent a week traversing the country on a luxury bus. We did fashion shoots in Colombo, the Cave Temple in Dambulla, atop the hills in Kandy and near the sea at Bentota.

As the editor, I was in charge of every detail, and relished the freedom that came with my position. Every night after work, I would jump into the hotel swimming pool and do a few laps. The lights at the bottom of the pool seemed as magical as the stars in the sky above me. The warm water lapped around my floating body, and feelings of awe flooded me. *I am here entirely of my own accord... I have created this opportunity for myself. I have made this happen, for myself, by myself...*

I basked in this euphoric haze for days after my return home.

My benevolent feelings towards mankind in general were disrupted by a phone call one night at 1 a.m.

'Hi, it's me,' said a male voice, breathless and urgent.

I glanced around groggily for my glasses, to check the caller ID. 'Who is this?'

There was a pause. 'Rajan—who else,' he said belligerently.

'Oh...Rajan...sorry,' I said, wondering why I was apologizing. What was so urgent that he had to disturb me at this late hour? 'Has something happened?'

There was a silence. 'Happened? What do you think has happened?' he snapped.

'No idea, Rajan...but something must be wrong, since you're calling at this unearthly hour,' I said, sitting up in bed.

'Haven't you wondered where I've been for the past two months, Ritu?'

I fumbled with my sheets, wide-awake now with shock. Was I being extra sensitive, or was his tone downright nasty?

'Listen Rajan, we aren't obliged to stay in touch with each other...you have your own life, and I have mine,' I said. 'I mean, we're just collegemates...friends...you know.'

Rajan laughed sarcastically. 'Really? Is that how you see our relationship...as a friendship without obligations?'

I was startled by his agitation. As always when in turmoil, my thoughts turned to sugar, and I wandered to the fridge to contemplate the contents. A packet of Ferrero Rocher chocolates beckoned me temptingly, and I pulled them out.

'Yes, Rajan, I think of you as a friend, someone I'd known in college.' I tore the wrapping off a chocolate and prodded it to check if it was soft enough to eat. The rush of sugar against the roof of my mouth combined with the crunchy nut at the centre, diminished the jarring effect of Rajan's tone.

'Well, Ritu, it's too bad that you see me as a "friend",' he said, sounding like a hurt child. 'And that it wouldn't matter to you, if we never met again.'

I was stunned. Why was Rajan being so dramatic? Where was the rational Rajan of my college days? Maybe his wife's mental illness had had an impact on him, and he was suffering from something similar to PTSD?

I popped another chocolate into my mouth and waited for the creaminess to work its magic.

'I have no idea why you're so worked up,' I said finally.

'Just forget what I said, Ritu,' he went on, 'and I will also forget I ever met you.' His voice dropped towards the end of his delivery, sounding almost forlorn.

Inexplicably, I started feeling guilty. 'Why don't you just tell me what the problem is, Rajan,' I prompted.

There was an audible sigh. 'I am mad about you,' he confessed. 'I told my face reader about you, and he did an aura reading to predict the future of our relationship.'

My mouth fell open. I started protesting. *What's wrong with you? Where did you get the idea that it was okay to have feelings for me? That I would even consider getting involved with you, a married man?*

I really hadn't anticipated this situation. What signs and signals had I missed? My naivety in assuming that my relationship with Rajan was simply an extension of our past friendship suddenly seemed idiotic and despicable. All those confessions and telephone calls obviously meant more to him than I'd imagined. Yet again, my helpful, open nature had led a man to think I was in love with him, simply because he was admitted into an easy camaraderie.

It wasn't the first time that a man with whom I wanted only friendship, thought I wanted sex or love from him. This really annoyed me, because I enjoyed the company of so many men who didn't attract me romantically. Surely I could 'hang out' with them just as I did with my women friends? So far, this hadn't worked too well, since I usually ended up trying to fend the guys off.

'You give off the wrong vibes,' said a friend, when I asked her what I was doing wrong. Now, here I was, all over again, in a messy situation of my own making.

'I'm flattered, Rajan,' I said sharply. 'But not interested in anything other than a friendship with you.'

There was a long silence. 'Why did you lead me on then…you're such a tease,' Rajan said, in a dangerously low voice.

'Look, Rajan…I had no idea,' I began.

But he cut me short and kept up his monotone. 'My wife had another manic episode—after she found out about us—and things have been very unpleasant at home,' he said.

'Found out…about us?' I repeated, hysterically. 'What's there to find out? I'm just a friend…we're just friends.'

I wanted to get up and rush over to explain everything to his wife. I was horrified that she could imagine I reciprocated her husband's interest in me, or think me capable of having an affair with him.

Rajan didn't care about my feelings though. 'I told Tulsi that, but she didn't believe me…she probably guessed how attracted I was to you.'

I was stunned that he had deliberately or inadvertently misled his wife into believing I was involved with him!

'Attracted to me?' I said, my voice rising angrily. 'Did you really think I was interested in you romantically?'

Rajan laughed sarcastically. 'Don't feign innocence,' he said. 'You gave me your number, invited me to your apartment and offered me a drink.'

⁓

Single women are always being hit on, everyone says. They are fair game for all men—young, old or infirm. Indeed, single women turn men from normal blokes into predators. So many episodes proved this to be true. Every time I had a bad experience, I felt the weight of the prejudice directed at women like me: ... *divorced women are easy game... no Indian man takes a single woman of your age seriously... it's your fault for making yourself available.*

The Rajan episode was the first of many, which involved married men. Neena was right after all: most of them assumed I was available, because I was single. The others chased me just because they believed it was their right to bed as many women as they liked. They were men, after all. And men could have as many sexual and romantic relationships as they wanted.

I remember one justification a married man-friend of mine provided for his numerous extramarital affairs. 'Arre, Krishna had hundreds of wives. History is full of gods with their gopis... and artists like Picasso who enjoyed multiple sexual relationships, everyone accepts it.'

His narcissism was striking, but not unusual.

But to me, being a target for married men was utterly offensive for many reasons: the assumption of my 'availability'; the direct, lewd manner in which they approached me; the threatening quality of their overtures; and their obvious disrespect for their wives, and the institution of marriage.

And I had no idea how to stop them in their tracks, since the majority were colleagues, or people within my friends' circle. Whenever I tried to discuss how to deal with these unwanted sexual advances, I was flummoxed by people's reactions.

'No big deal,' said a male relative. 'All men are like that.'

In fact, the that's-how-men-are justifications were everyone's favourite. From times immemorial, the sexual misbehaviour of men was blamed on their biology: male sexual urges, said everyone, are enormous and uncontrollable. The theory was that the penis had a life of its own, unconnected to the rational mind.

Even well-educated women I met subscribed to this assumption. 'Men can't help themselves,' said an eminent lady psychologist I interviewed at that time, for an article on sexual harassment.

I realized I must have bought into this assumption. Despite my outrage at the manner in which men used their power and position to harass me, I felt powerless to stop them. Tackling male propositioning just became one of the new challenges of my single life. So, I converted it into a source of entertainment. In the beginning, I treated all overtures like a game. The first question I asked every married guy who propositioned me after the Rajan episode, was, 'So, what's in it for me? After all, your wife enjoys the benefits of being a married woman. What would I get out of being with you?'

Their responses varied from 'mind-blowing sex' to

'holidays in Goa' and 'good work opportunities'. Obviously, they imagined that any one of all these 'prizes' would suffice for a single woman of my age. Something was better than nothing, after all. Here I was, a woman who watched *Grey's Anatomy* by herself five nights a week. Naturally I would be grateful for the attention of a (any) man, who would distract me from my TV show and lighten up my life, with his occasional foray into my bed.

It never struck any of the guys who approached me that TV offered me better company than them. Or that I wouldn't have chosen them even when I was young, or if they were single.

~

Most of the married guys who made a pass at me were simply looking for a distraction from their evidently dull marital relationships. A little action on the side with a woman like me (who had no right to expect anything much from them or life in general) posed the ideal solution for their sleepy sex lives: they were doing me a favour really.

Their approach was usually direct, since they had no intention of wasting time or money on courting me—lewd text messages, emails and on one occasion, when a guy walked me home from a dinner party, the suggestion, straight off, that we should head to my bedroom. 'Listen, I'm in an open marriage,' he declared, with the brashness of a teenager making an ill-timed move on his girlfriend.

Once, I accepted a colleague, Sanjay's, invitation for a drink, imagining that socializing with a co-worker and family man was no big deal. I got this grand idea from yet another of my favourite TV shows, *Ali McBeal*, which was about lawyers and their lives, and ended with a scene set in a bar with music, with all the male and female lawyers drinking together and discussing their cases and life philosophies.

I imagined Sanjay and I would do the same; discuss the politics of the newspaper we worked for, and exchange notes on music and books. I was in for a rude shock though, since Sanjay was clear that the only thing he wanted from me was sex. His lines were similar to those I'd heard from others. *My marriage is a sham; I stay just for the children.*

Sanjay vented his frustration over the way his wife raised the kids, her erratic spending habits, the lack of cleanliness at home, and how dull everything between them had become. He told me I was bright and beautiful, and that he had to 'have' me. 'You don't know what you're missing,' he said, when I turned him down.

But that didn't stop him from trying again and again. Sanjay just wouldn't take no for an answer. We were alone in the conference room when he propositioned me for the third time.

'No one needs to know about it,' he whispered, glancing through the glass to make sure that none of our co-workers were within listening distance.

Instead of calling him out on his behaviour, I engineered a situation that put him in a corner. 'That will be impossible for me,' I stated, collecting my papers and putting them in a pile, 'since my life is an open book. So if we're going to have a relationship, then everyone should know.'

I looked him directly in the eye and went on. 'Living

alone is really hard, so I will need you around a lot of the time, to supervise plumbers, electricians and carpenters. Maybe you could even help with my tax return...I would probably need your car and driver a few times a week too.'

I could see Sanjay visibly shrinking as I jabbered on. He looked more and more frightened. But the sentence that provided me a sure line of escape, was my declaration that I was unwilling to be the 'other woman'.

'I don't believe in secrecy,' I said firmly, 'so your wife would have to know.'

My strategy worked. He avoided me thereafter. He got away, believing that he was the one who had opted out. In the typical way of women of my generation, I let him think that, knowing that I had appeased him instead of exposing his behaviour. My need to keep things pleasant and avoid creating a hostile atmosphere at the office for myself, won over. Today, I regret my lack of courage: I should have taken the matter to the HR department of the office, or told Sanjay off in front of our colleagues.

This incident forced me to accept how hesitant I was to confront men for breaching boundaries with me. Despite my emancipation, I hesitated to stick labels where they belonged: cheater or adulterer or addict or loser. Obviously, I wasn't alone in my male-protective stance: I've witnessed dozens of women behaving like I did, making excuses for the wrongdoings of men. Fear aside, it's the compulsive need to be nice that keeps women from protesting against unwanted sexual advances. The question is, unless we label it in our heads, how can we proclaim it in public?

10

Mr Middle-aged and His Mummy Are Never Parted

'Are there any charming, funny, confident men who truly love women?' inquired friends curious about the outcome of my search for romance. Yes, I replied, but I haven't met them yet. The middle-aged men I'd encountered so far were pleasant enough, even though they didn't shake my world. Their attitudes to romantic relationships varied from a 'been there, done that' stance, to a more earnest 'would be great to meet someone new' one.

A man who'd lost his wife in a car accident couldn't stop reminiscing about their wonderful marriage, and two divorced men still had close friendships with their ex-wives. I met a few men who were separated from their wives, but didn't express any intentions of divorcing them.

I took a fancy to a publisher, in the 'separated' category, who seemed keen on me too. 'You must come by for a drink,' he said, on more than one occasion. I was tempted. But his constant 'my wife' references put me off: *my wife used to say that I'm too impulsive, my wife used to say that broccoli is best eaten steamed, my wife used to say that I need to exercise more...*

It seemed unlikely that he would ever contemplate a serious relationship with any other woman. Like others in his situation, he used his defunct marriage as a shield. His ambivalence reflected the general lackadaisical attitude towards romantic relationships, which I sensed in the men of my generation: it was as if they were immune to changing social mores, and the new landscape of relationships between the sexes.

Culturally and mythologically, mid-life is the beginning of old age and decline for Indians: crossing the age of forty-five signals the onset of 'winnowing', the time to shed whatever your soul doesn't need, and forsake your sensuality. Middle-aged Indians are meant to have moved beyond the fantasies of youth and romance. But popular culture today contradicts the traditional Indian view of mid-life. Media images suggest that being forty or fifty doesn't signal the end of romantic and sexual possibilities. Instead, this is the age of possibilities, the onset of a second puberty.

A movie icon like 52-year-old Bollywood star Salman Khan embodies the new aspirations of mid-life, with his muscular arms, pelvic thrusts and stream of young, sexy girlfriends to prove his virility. Hollywood stars like Madonna and Sharon Stone echo the same message for women: hit the gym and defy gravity, slather on crème de la mer, get a new attitude and mate with a much younger man, to stay young.

Even New Age gurus espouse the notion of 'the new mid-life', calling it a 'magical turning point towards life as we've never known it.' Bestselling author of *The Age of Miracles*, Marianne Williamson, says we need to stop regarding mid-life as a crisis. 'Treat it like a time of rebirth,' she advises. Being a fan of her books, I took her advice seriously, making up my mind to 'reinvent' myself.

I fell for the pitch of a Bruce Lee-style trainer, who convinced me that his workout would 'transform' me.

Naturally, the fantasy of a new, lean body was irresistible. Every morning for four months, I sweated through a gruelling regime of push-ups, squats, crunches and weight-training. To my disappointment, my body barely registered any change.

Still, this wasn't the end of my pursuit of a New Me. I succumbed next to the sales pitch of a laser-happy dermatologist with gelled hair, whom I met at a press conference on skin therapies. Dr Derma managed to convince me that laser therapy held the secret to my youth, and had the power to change my future.

'These babies are the answer to your dreams,' he said, stroking the laser machines lying beside him.

Dr Derma was passionately attached to his lasers, and drove around with a couple of portable ones in the back seat of his car. It wasn't possible to doubt his intentions. The first time I consulted him, he reached out across his desk and patted my cheeks. It would have been considered an intimate gesture if it came from anyone other than a dermatologist.

'Smile so I can see your crow's feet,' he commanded. 'Raise your eyebrows and let me check the damage on your brow.' This set the tone of our relationship.

Dr Derma persuaded me to spend a fat sum of money on a laser facelift, which he insisted would take a decade off my face. I fell for it. I lay flat on my back, on the narrow bed in his tiny basement clinic and let him smear gels onto the contours of my face. He administered 300 pulses of the laser. They were like shock waves.

I constantly checked my reflection in a magnifying mirror for six months after this treatment, to try and assess the difference. I kept waiting for some other woman (or man) to tell me I looked fantastic, and say, 'My God, what have you done to yourself?' or something similar.

But nothing of the kind happened. Yet, Dr Derma wouldn't stop selling me ways to attain a new, youthful appearance. He had a fresh suggestion every week.

'Hi Ritu, is there any fat you want removed—from your upper arms, or thighs?' he said one time.

The next was, 'Hi Ritu, are there any pits or freckles on your face you want to get rid of?'

I recommended him to friends, to get him off my back. They loved him. They said he was taking care of their every blemish, every bit of patchy skin or discolouration on their faces or necks or wherever. They paid him huge sums for sessions with his beautiful lasers, to get rid of their pesky problems. I would have made a fortune, too, if I'd asked for a commission!

~

The theme of falling in love and starting over again at mid-life is also popular in films and books.

Bollywood has the 2005 *Pyaar Mein Twist*, in which two middle-aged single parents (Dimple Kapadia and Rishi Kapoor) fall in love during their children's marriage. Watching 64-year-old Amitabh Bachchan wooing 34-year-old Tabu in the 2007 film *Cheeni Kum* also suggests that it's never too late to fall in love. Indeed, a second, third and fourth life awaits you, even if divorce or bereavement has staked an early claim to the first. This new, refreshing view of middle age, in reel life, at least, offers us the chance to reinvent our personalities, discover new love and change our destinies.

But, in real life, switching gears and changing track in mid-life is easier said than done for the men of my generation. How to start afresh? Many men I talked to were unsure whether they wanted, or needed, a new, serious romantic relationship in mid-life. So they moved back into a bedroom of their parents' houses after a separation, divorce or bereavement. Why set up an independent establishment, when it was so much easier to live unencumbered by responsibilities?

Middle-aged men who moved into parental homes fell back into childhood patterns. They kept their romantic and sexual pursuits out of the house. Widowed mothers ruled, and the guys used Mama as a means of distracting themselves from their own empty personal lives.

Ajit was one such person. I met him at a friend B's farewell party. Men were clustered in one corner discussing politics and investments, and women exchanged notes on their children, maids, and tailors. I spotted an empty seat on the sofa, beside a fair, mousy-looking man, and sat down, giving him a tentative smile. He smiled back, leaning towards me, poised for a conversation.

We introduced ourselves. The doorbell kept ringing; the sounds of laughter, chatter, music and the excited barking of B's dog was nearly deafening. This didn't matter to Ajit, since he was determined to be heard.

'This party scene is all new to me,' he said, gesturing at the room and popping peanuts noisily into his mouth. 'You see I've only just come back to this country. I've lived in Sydney for most of my life.'

Ajit said that things had been much quieter in the old days in India. There was less consumerism; no malls, no cable TV and none of the flashiness that was visible now.

'Delhi's so junked up!' he complained. He really missed the natural beauty of Australia and was struggling to get used to being in this rowdy city. Worse still, he was stuck here indefinitely, since his mother was in her eighties and needed him around.

I kept nodding and tried to listen politely, even though I longed to sip my beer and sit back. The day had been long and tiring and being forced to pay attention to Ajit's litany of woes was exhausting.

'Kya kare... mummy insists I stay with her,' he went on. Being the only son and heir of a huge house in a posh locality of Delhi was serious business. He had to hang around and stake a claim to his inheritance.

'I've heard all these scary stories about how relatives manage to get hold of houses in Delhi,' he said. Living with his mother seemed a small price to pay. At least that's what he imagined, before he moved in with her.

'She treats me like a child, barging into my room to check on me... she insists on accompanying me each time I go out,' he said mournfully.

Miraculously, Santana's rhythm filled the room. *Don't turn your back on me baby... Don't turn your back on me baby...* I sat back and sighed with pleasure, recalling the lusty feelings 'Black Magic Woman' aroused in me when I was growing up. I would put it on ten times a day, and wiggle around my bedroom to the beat, checking myself out in the full-length mirror on my cupboard. I pouted and preened, imagining the soulful Santana rocking beside me, in tune with my movements.

Ajit's leg had flopped against mine. I shifted, to break body contact. I needn't have worried though, since his action was involuntary. In fact, there were no signs that he'd even registered the fact that I had a leg, or any other body parts. I could have been a part of the sofa, for all he cared. 'You know, mum wants me to report all my comings and goings to her,' he droned on.

Nothing he said was new or unusual. For a long time, I had heard similar accounts from friends about how their parents and in-laws overstepped their boundaries. Anyone born in an Indian family knows that they will be treated like a child by their parents forever, regardless of their age. I thumped my tepid glass of beer down on the peg table impatiently.

'Maybe you should find a place of your own, Ajit,' I said unsympathetically. 'And get a life of your own.'

He looked hurt, and moved away from me. 'That's easy for you to say,' he snapped. 'You have no idea about the responsibilities of a man.'

I stood up, appalled. Here was a guy who had bored me for the past hour with his conversation, hadn't asked a single question about my life, and now believed he had the right to pass judgment on me!

Other interactions with middle-aged desi guys have convinced me that whatever little interest they had in other people, has slowly dissipated over the years. Their conversations revolve around the nitty-gritty of their own lives; ageing parents, ex-wives, children (if they have any); official positions they hold or have held in the past; property and political matters, and the like.

Once they warm up to you, all their secret health

issues emerge. Apart from their battle with an expanding girth, there's a host of lifestyle ailments that crop up at this stage of life: cardiac problems, high BP, enlarged prostate, reflux, diabetes, backaches—not to mention insomnia, and snoring, which is endemic. I know at least two men who sleep hooked up to machines that supply oxygen that they lose due to sleep apnea. The prospect of sharing their beds is distinctly unappealing.

Like Ajit, I met other older singles who lived with one or both parents and appeared abnormally attached to, and simultaneously antagonistic towards them. They thrived on complaining about the travails of their living arrangement. But they never mentioned moving out.

Regardless of their age, Indian guys rarely stray far from the parental nest. They feel a moral compulsion to 'look after' their parents. Their attachment to their parents isn't always entirely altruistic, though; there are properties and businesses to be inherited, and desi boys will go to great length to ensure that they don't lose out on anything.

No woman should underestimate the hold of an Indian man's family on his life, or the emotional web cast by mothers on their sons. A former classmate, Jia, was enraged that her 48-year-old man-friend wouldn't marry her because his mother was opposed to the union. 'It's ridiculous how his mummy dictates his life even at his age!' she complained.

Indeed, Indian mothers resent having to retreat from their son's lives, and fight hard to keep the 'other' woman, like Jia, from claiming the emotional space they believe is exclusively theirs.

Though Jia's mate had a degree from Oxford and

appeared to be a progressive thinker, he didn't have the guts to strike out on his own.

'What difference does it make if we wait a little longer, till ma gets used to the idea,' he kept repeating, in an attempt to pacify her.

Jia called me some months later to tell me her pal had finally moved into an apartment, alone.

~

Some of the middle-aged men I met preferred the company of much younger women. They were blatant about their interest in quick, easy affairs, and enjoyment of sexual liaisons with whoever reciprocated their interest. Since they'd grown up at the same time as me, I guessed they'd had a conservative upbringing. But that didn't stop them from taking advantage of the 'sexually emancipated' new Indian woman—who was the subject of a wave of sex surveys appearing in news magazines like *India Today* and *Outlook*.

My encounter with Kartik, a guy I met at a personal growth workshop, was a real revelation in this regard. He was tall and lithe with salt and pepper hair, wore a pink shirt and shoes with white rubber soles. He laughed with an attractive abandon, and was also extremely forthright during the workshop, sharing all kinds of personal details about himself—how rejected he felt by his father, the insomnia that plagued him night after night, his addiction to gambling—the kind of stuff most of us try and hide.

I was charmed by his warmth and lack of reserve. Maybe there were some evolved guys out there after all. When Kartik strolled up to me during the tea break and suggested we keep in touch, I responded immediately, excited at the prospect of getting to know him better. The fact that I knew absolutely nothing about him didn't matter. He suggested lunch the following day. I shook my head regretfully, explaining that I had a job and wasn't free during the daytime. He asked where my office was. 'That's half a kilometre from my place,' he exclaimed when I told him. 'Why don't you drop by for tea on your way home?'

For a moment, I hesitated, wondering if meeting him at his house was appropriate. Though I'd invited men to my place before for coffee or lunch, just because it was convenient, I didn't want my decision to go to Kartik's house to be misunderstood. To my relief, Kartik put an end to my indecision, with his next statement.

'I live with my mother.'

The next evening, I parked my car in the park in front of Kartik's house. He was waiting outside, and greeted me warmly. He led me into a drawing room crowded by large, ornate wooden sofas and tables. I sat down gingerly on what appeared to be the most comfortable sofa. 'Lemon tea?' he suggested. Before I could reply, he yelled, 'Bahadur beta, lemon tea lao.'

A sulky-looking Nepalese boy popped his head out from the kitchen. A few moments later, an elderly woman wearing a smocked, flowery nightie wandered into the room. I smiled uncertainly, wondering if I should stand up to greet her.

But before I could get up, Kartik intervened. 'Relax, yaar... it's just mummy.' He ushered his mother to the seat beside mine. 'Come meet Ritu, mummy,' he said.

His mother beamed at me, moving closer to examine

my face. 'You look familiar…Weren't you eating chicken with some foreigner on one of those travel shows?'

Kartik looked flabbergasted. I burst out laughing at his expression and turned to his mum. 'Yes, I was…I appeared on a British travel show called *Paul Merton in India*,' I said.

'But why were you eating chicken?' asked Kartik, curiously.

'The episode was filmed over dinner,' I explained, telling them about the show, and how the scene was intended to draw attention to the host's lack of eating etiquette.

'He was an Englishman in India, who took an etiquette class to learn how to eat Indian food in the right manner, but ended up breaking the rules, holding the chicken wrong, things like that,' I elaborated.

Kartik's mother giggled, and then sighed. 'Well, the chicken looked tasty enough… and you looked gorgeous,' she chirped, 'I'm glad my son is entertaining a well-known lady, for a change.'

Kartik's expression turned black. 'What do you mean by that, mummy? Don't give Ritu the wrong impression,' he snapped.

His mother ignored him, and asked me where I lived. We chatted for a while, and then she got up to leave, saying she had to supervise dinner preparations.

'She likes you,' Kartik said, nodding approvingly at me, '…which is rare, since she mostly disapproves of the ladies who come over.'

I leaned back on the sofa, unsure of how to react: should I be pleased that the mother of a guy I'd known for just about an hour liked me, or not? Or should I feel let down that he had plenty of ladies over?

Kartik pulled out a cigarette from his pocket and pointed it at me. 'You don't mind, do you, sweetie?'

I shrugged. There was no point in saying I hated being called sweetie by a man I barely knew, or that I was hardly at liberty to ask him not to smoke, in his own house. In any case, he had already lit up.

After a few drags, he started telling me about his life: he was forty when his wife passed away after a two-year struggle with breast cancer, leaving him to raise their ten-year-old son. Kartik moved in with his widowed mother at that point. 'There was no way I could bring up a kid by myself,' he explained.

I nodded, and told him about my own son, who was around the same age as his. 'Luckily his father looks after him as well as I do, so I'm not a single parent,' I declared.

Right from the start, I had accepted how much L needed his father's presence in his life. The limitations of my independent existence were also obvious. So, L divided his time between his father's place and mine. It wasn't an easy arrangement, but it had worked so far.

Kartik looked perplexed. 'But how do you manage to co-parent living in two houses?' he asked.

'He has a bedroom in both houses,' I responded abruptly. Kartik took the cue and dropped the subject.

Kartik lit up another cigarette and inhaled deeply, blowing out smoke in a spiral. 'So what's your love life been like?' he said, giving me a meaningful look. 'Rocking, haan?'

'Why don't you tell me about yours—it's bound to be more interesting than mine,' I countered, sure he wouldn't pass up the opportunity to talk about himself.

He stood up and began pacing the room. After flicking the ash off his smoke, he confessed to several short-lived relationships with women, none of which had blossomed into anything permanent.

'Why is that?' I asked curiously.

'The last woman I was with, Meghna, caught me in bed with someone else,' he said. 'It was just sex, yaar… the other woman meant nothing. But Meghna wouldn't believe me.' There was a note of pride rather than regret in his voice.

I sighed in dismay. Lately I'd begun wondering if the tendency to disclose personal details—often of an inappropriate, sexual nature—too soon in a relationship was characteristic of Indian men in particular? It was a clumsy opening move, if that is what it was intended to be.

Kartik was oblivious to my discomfort though, and plodded on with his sordid tale. After a few feeble attempts at 'serious' relationships with women his age—ostensibly with the idea of remarrying—Kartik discovered it was easier to have brief flings with young women who expected nothing from him, except a well-stuffed wallet.

I wasn't surprised to hear this, since much was being made in the media about the 'hook up' culture that had gained momentum. One-night stands were apparently the norm among Indian teens looking for quick physical pleasure, in place of long-term commitment. Just weeks ago, a pornographic MMS made by two students of Delhi Public School, was widely circulated after being illegally auctioned on eBay India. Entitled 'DPS Girls Having Fun', this sex clip had scandalized middle-class parents.

'I was a timepass for young, hot babes—an older guy

who took them out for coffee, beer, movies, bought them gifts in exchange for their company and casual sex, of course,' said Kartik. These flings were much easier than a serious romantic relationship, which involved more emotional investment than he was ready for.

The problem was that his formula had stopped working since his business crashed. There was less money to throw around on women. Also, his ageing was visible, despite hours spent in the gym. 'I've been thinking that maybe it's time to hang around with women my own age, you know what I mean?' he drawled.

I sat back and absorbed his story, feeling like something heavy had been dropped on my head. Was it the fashionable thing for men to bombard women they were romantically interested in, with information that was possibly detrimental to their relationship?

But Kartik hadn't finished. 'Since you also have a son,' he said conversationally, 'let me ask you what you did about his sex education, sweetie?' I was aghast, and decided the guy really had the brain of a pea. 'Only foolish parents think they need to provide their kids sex education,' I said dismissively. 'My son must have picked up whatever he knows from his pals or TV... or maybe some girl.'

Kartik looked at me with disbelief. 'How can you be so irresponsible?' he muttered.

I switched off, and began looking around for something to distract me from the conversation. A tapestry of pansies on the wall caught my eye. It was so intricate. I began wondering who had made it. Could it be his mother? How long would it take to do this embroidery? Five days?

I got up to get a closer look, and mused about how knitting and embroidery had become literally extinct. The world we women inhabited today was so different from that of our mothers and grandmothers. The hours, days and weeks spent creating a tapestry of such beauty are simply not justifiable any longer. We have to prove ourselves constantly, juggling the roles of daughter, mother, wife, employee. Unless we are superwomen, though, we can't live up to the expectations laden on us by our families, friends and society.

Kartik's agitated voice intruded upon my reverie. 'How can you be so casual about sex education, in this day and age?' he was saying. 'All good parents—especially mothers—know how important it is to teach their kids to protect themselves.'

I felt my indignation rising. Who was he to comment on my mothering skills?

'Oh come on, man—there's enough information floating around… the girls teach the boys everything about sex these days—there's TV—internet—we hardly need to spoonfeed our kids these days,' I countered.

My ill-thought out response was a mistake, since it provided him precisely the opportunity he wanted. 'I bought my son two tapes you know—one demonstrating condom use and the second one on how to handle intimate relationships.'

'That's great, Kartik, I'm happy for you,' I said sharply, standing up and picking up my handbag.

'What's the hurry? You've only just come,' he said, trying to block my way. I brushed past him, to the front door. His mother reappeared from somewhere. She had discarded the nightie for a pink chiffon saree. 'You're going already, Ritu? I was just about to make some pakoras for you,' she said, 'though I'm sure you'd prefer a piece of chicken!'

I laughed and thanked her for the thought. 'Your handiwork is amazing,' I said, indicating the pansy picture. She looked confused, but smiled anyway.

I let my distaste with Kartik sink in on the drive home. Maybe I was overreacting. The prissy side of my nature surprised me: maybe his constant references to sex put me off, because he belonged to my generation, had schooled at Doon and probably grown up with a handbook of manners? Whatever the reason, I couldn't get rid of the bad feeling in my mouth.

But he hadn't picked up on my reaction, and called me incessantly over the following week. I responded once, in an attempt to be polite. That was a mistake. 'Let's go for a movie tonight, nah,' Kartik said. 'Let's go and see *No Entry*—everyone's talking about it.' I told him I already had plans for the evening. He sent me a bouquet of red gladiolas a few days later. I sent him a message of thanks, but didn't respond to his phone calls.

~

Premature retirement was the privilege of many South Delhi men, I discovered. They lived off rental income and investments, and spent their days flitting between various activities: watching cricket, keeping elderly parents company, walking up and down from neighbourhood marketplaces and banks, golfing or drinking at clubs.

They seemed quite happy frittering away their time

in this manner, and were disinterested in getting deeply involved in any project, or learning anything new. Their lives seemed to have halted, prematurely, limiting their aspirations and interests. I tried to tell myself that they epitomized the 'being' advocated in Buddhist teachings, but this rationalization didn't make it easier for me to have a conversation with them.

Roop was one such guy. I met him for the first time at the Star supermarket, while I was debating between buying green tea with mint or lemongrass.

'Excuse me,' said a tall grey-haired man with gold-rimmed spectacles. 'I hope you don't mind my asking… but are you Arundhati Roy?'

I put the mint tea back on its shelf, and looked at him sideways. 'No, I'm not,' I said dismissively. What a bizarre pick-up line, that too from an elderly man! I began examining the South Indian fast food mixes. Mr Gold Rims picked up the MTR brand vada packet and waved it at me. 'Take this one—it's the best,' he said, planting himself firmly in my path.

Roop, short for Rupinder, wore tight jeans and a red shirt, which were an odd contrast to his mop of grey hair. He told me he had moved to Delhi some months earlier, after a thirty-year stint in the US. 'My parents begged me to come back,' he said. His mother was suffering from Alzheimer's and his father was too frail to look after her.

Since he was back for good, he'd decided to resettle. He was on the lookout for a woman to marry, and was enjoying doing the social rounds. Like other widowed or divorced men, he was still considered eligible (unlike single women his age) and had no dearth of dinner invitations.

'What about you, Ritu, are you happily wed?'

I laughed nervously, and made up some story about a husband. Our brief interaction was enough to set off warning bells in my head, and I had no desire to fuel his romantic interest.

But there was no avoiding him. He was all over the neighbourhood—in parks, at fruit vendors, and paying telephone and electricity bills at the local offices. Roop was always upbeat and ready for a chat. 'That's what I like about being in India,' he'd say gregariously. 'There's always someone to talk to.'

He was curious about me, in a limited way. His interest was high when I talked about plumbers, electricians and the best places for upholstery shopping. But he avoided venturing into any world he was not familiar with. So, the moment I started talking about why the public health system needed overhauling or mentioned a book I enjoyed reading, he switched off.

His own routine was fixed, and centered on a predictable set of activities. He read only the *Hindustan Times*, watched only the NDTV news, bought mithai only from Evergreen Sweets in Green Park, and spent every Tuesday morning at the temple. Literature, art, culture, history and science didn't enter his world, and he was quite content with the daily stuff of life.

Like other prematurely retired men, Roop dismissed my career, since it was too hard for him to acknowledge that I contributed something to a world he had dropped out of. Though he was aware that I was a writer, worked with a newspaper and edited a weekly health supplement, he never read anything I wrote. Work was a dirty word for him and he couldn't comprehend my interest in mine. But I took great pleasure in telling him how much I enjoyed my job, and making money. Though he would have been more comfortable with me minimizing my accomplishments, I took perverse pleasure in doing the opposite.

Still, Roop kept trying to divert the conversation to something he was comfortable with, such as his charitable deeds: how he'd taken his maid's daughter to the doctor when she was ill and supplied her with milk, fruit and nuts till she recovered; how he had to make two trips to Lajpat Nagar for his father's vests; how he insisted on buying an elderly aunt a washing machine. He was undoubtedly a do-gooder, but I enjoyed his stories about his escapades involving his search for a 'suitable woman' more than those attesting to his goodness.

∼

Six months after our supermarket encounter, Roop suggested we have a bite at Big Chill Cafe. I agreed, having labelled him 'harmless' by now.

Over tomato basil soup, he updated me on his search for a matrimonial partner and how lonely he was.

I murmured understandingly. 'So what kind of person are you looking for?' I ventured, savouring the garlic bread.

Roop looked pensive. 'A cultured, good-looking lady willing to help look after my parents,' he said decisively.

I was bemused: Why not just hire a nurse instead, I thought to myself.

But Roop fancied himself as a grand catch for any woman. He was convinced that the city was flush with women who would benefit from his financial support and companionship. There was so much on offer: enough money to live comfortably, an apartment in South Delhi, a car and driver, and plenty of time at his disposal to take a wife shopping or travelling.

Surely, any woman would be grateful, and willing to care for Roop's parents in exchange. 'No woman could bargain for a better life than what I can offer,' he proclaimed.

I bit my tongue to stop my sarcastic retort, and exhaled slowly. Maybe his pomposity wasn't entirely his fault, since his mother and probably plenty of other women too, led him to believe that he was a gift to womanhood.

Still, his tales of lusty encounters with a stream of women keen on hooking him were entertaining enough.

'Everybody knows that I'm on the lookout,' Roop informed me, and his social life had really taken off ever since he announced his intention to marry. He spent many evenings at lavish dinner parties hosted by well-to-do friends, at farms and fancy restaurants. Also, he was part of a movie-going group.

The only problem, he said, was that married women had started hitting on him too. Last week, he'd had to fend off the overtures of a lady called Nina, who showed up at his front door, unannounced.

'I was on my way to the bakery and suddenly remembered you lived around the corner,' she simpered.

Though taken aback, he recovered quickly and invited her in for a cup of coffee. 'I was just being polite,' Roop explained to me.

Two nights later, Nina had called him up. 'Can I come over now—I really need to talk to you,' she said, in a husky undertone.

'I was terrified, yaar—she has a burly sardar husband who would beat me to a pulp if he thought there was any hanky-panky going on,' he said. So, Roop said no, but Nina wouldn't listen and he was forced to agree to a meeting at a coffee shop.

Nina arrived in a low-cut, lacy blouse that revealed her ample bosom. She thanked him for coming and put her hand over his.

'Look, Roop, I am very unhappy with the sardarji...,' she began.

Roop tried to cut her short. 'What's wrong with you? What makes you imagine I'm interested in your marital problems,' he said sternly.

Nina's expression became coy. 'You are getting the wrong idea, Roop... all I want from you is a little affection,' she declared, 'without strings.'

Roop claimed to be shocked. 'She even suggested we rent a room in a guesthouse run by a friend of hers, can you believe it, Ritu?'

As far as I could tell, Roop was averse to the suggestion only because of the threat of Nina's husband. He didn't seem to mind her sexual interest in him—judging by the gloat in his voice when he told me about it.

⁓

The spoiler in my conversations with Roop was the constant digs he took at his ex-wife. His verbal barrage against his ex always made me uncomfortable. 'She was a real bitch, who hated my parents,' he said bitterly. 'She wouldn't let them come and visit me... or shop for them... she even tried to stop me from caring for them when they were ill...'

I kept trying to think of ways to steer the dialogue in another direction. Once someone got going on the topic of their exes, the conversation generally went downhill. And I'd come to realize that a man's description of his relationship break-ups—and whether or not he claimed his share of responsibility for the failure—was an indicator of his maturity.

As I listened to Roop drone on, I recalled the remarks of other men about lovers, female friends, ex-girlfriends, even sisters and mothers. These usually reflected their general views and feelings for women.

~

Every time we met, Roop updated me on the status of his partner search. When I asked him whether he had put his profile up on an online marriage site, he scoffed at me. 'Why would someone like me need to do that!' The truth was that Roop hadn't put his profile up on an online matchmaking site, because he had no idea how to use a computer.

'There's absolutely no need for a computer in my life,' was his response when I suggested he buy one and learn to use it. His attitude reflected his general laziness and resistance to change. But he clearly enjoyed telling me about his romantic escapades. Many times I wondered how many of his stories were fabrications or exaggerations: the women he talked about seemed so desperate and conniving. He described Sheena, a bubbly divorcee with a 15-year-old daughter, who claimed to be in her forties.

Roop didn't believe her. During one of their outings, he managed to get his hands on her driving licence and discovered she was fifty-four.

'If she can lie so blatantly to me about her age, who knows what else she is lying about,' he declared.

When I pressed him for details about how he got hold of her licence in the first place, he was evasive. 'Her bag fell down and I was picking up the contents when I saw it,' he said, averting his eyes.

Another woman who was very 'tall and good-looking' pressed him to move to the US with her. 'Let's start afresh,' she urged.

Roop was affronted. 'How stupid is she? She knows I'm committed to caring for my parents.'

A year after we met, Roop admitted that his search for a wife was heading nowhere.

'Why don't you look for a girlfriend instead,' I suggested. 'Someone who's independent, has her own set up, and is content to be your companion?'

Roop's face lit up. 'What a great idea, Ritu...you know I've liked you from the moment we met.'

I shook my head vigorously, and blurted out what I'd been longing to, from the moment we met. 'Roop, you're very nice, but I'm not interested in you that way.'

11

The World of HIV and Intellectual Men

Five years into my single life, I still hadn't resolved the issue of how to make a stable livelihood. Though I'd had some lucrative assignments and part-time jobs, there were periods when these dried up. And the question of what to do next always plagued me: when my energy was high, I'd write letters and make calls to everyone I knew, for leads. Sometimes this worked, and I got a report to write, a conference to report on, or some case studies. At that time the development sector was flush with funds for HIV/AIDS, since everyone had decided that India was in the throes of an HIV/AIDS epidemic.

Sometimes, I was offered jobs for which I had no formal training. Once, I was commissioned to do an article on the occasion of World AIDS day, in a drug de-addiction centre, where I planned to interview some of the inmates who had tested positive for HIV. The founder of the Sunshine Center, Elizabeth, was a charismatic and lively woman of my age. We developed an instant rapport with each other, and soon after we met, she called and asked me to do some case studies of her pet project: a rehabilitation centre for women and children.

'We can't pay you much, but your inputs would be greatly appreciated,' she said.

I agreed to visit the women's centre to check out the

scope of work. It was located just outside the city, facing a forest area. The first time I went there, I saw a group of desolate-looking women sitting on the floor of the long verandah that opened into a dusty courtyard. Some took long drags from their bidis. Others sat in a stupor, staring out onto the horizon. Empty packets of pan masala and bidis lay blowing in the wind. A mangy-looking dog was being chased by two little children.

'That's what hopelessness looks like,' said Elizabeth matter-of-factly.

When I began recording case studies, I discovered the varied backgrounds of the residents: most came to the centre for de-addiction and rehabilitation, but others had HIV and mental illnesses too. Medical and personal histories of the residents had been recorded in a haphazard way, and many had unidentified illnesses. Large chunks of their life stories hadn't been recorded, and when I went through their files, I learned that almost every single woman had suffered some sort of abuse. Their stories were complicated and fascinating.

Strangely enough, they didn't hold back from recounting their often sordid pasts. The HIV positive women lived at the edge. They had lost almost everything, including their children, who were being raised by extended families. All that was left to do was to take anti-retrovirals and survive as long as their bodies allowed.

For the addicts, drug use, prostitution, lying, manipulating, theft and violence were basic tools of survival. Most of the women had been abused by fathers, brothers and lovers and turned to drugs, as an act of rebellion or just to keep the men in their lives company. Their tales were gruesome and kept me awake at night.

I wracked my brain for solutions to their problems. What could they do to improve their lives? Even if they managed to kick their drug habit and chuck their miserable relationships, what next? There was no escaping the fact that big moves needed economic and emotional backing of some kind. My inability to come up with any concrete suggestions was frustrating.

When I discussed the women and their problems with my close circle, they expressed concern. 'How can you work in such a place?' said a perplexed friend. 'There's the risk of contracting any kind of infection… and then you're dealing with women from a totally different background and life experience. How can you even relate to them?'

The answer to her question was simple. Women's lives are more similar than we imagine, and I was spellbound by the facets that bound us. They were misfits in their own lives, just the way I was. Their stories were about love and losses, and the absence of any real opportunities to discover their own needs or strengths, just like mine.

Some were real love junkies, who had spent most of their lives in search of that 'special' relationship, to distract them from their chaotic inner worlds and fear of being alone. So far, the course of their lives had been determined by the men they lived with. Ironically the very men they depended upon had pushed them into drug addiction!

Regardless of their socio-economic backgrounds, several women felt ill-suited to the roles thrust upon them. Drug addiction was a response to the pressure some felt, about conforming to gender expectations. One said that being a drug user enabled her to escape her role as a homemaker, and share the rough culture of the street with her husband instead, which made her more of a man.

Another said she abhorred the daily, repetitive tasks that came with being a wife and mother. 'I'm not interested in keeping my house clean and looking after my child,' she declared defiantly, half expecting me to admonish her. How could I? I knew exactly how she felt, and how lonely it was to be a stray in the tribe.

I also knew that regardless of differences, everyone wanted love, security and acceptance.

～

I wrote a series of features about HIV/AIDS for national newspapers. These highlighted the misconceptions about how the virus was transmitted, and the discrimination suffered by those who tested positive. I was hooked by the tales of sex workers who'd contracted HIV though clients; monogamous housewives whose husbands had infected them and drug addicts who'd got the virus through shared needles. Everyone was struggling to reconcile their losses.

My articles were well received, and one day I had a job offer from a British NGO, Health Matters (HM). I accepted it immediately, since my bank account was totally depleted. As the communications manager of HM, I was supposed to advocate for a number of health-related causes: oral rehydration treatment (ORT) for children with diarrhoeal diseases, water purification tablets to ensure safe water, and condoms to avert HIV and other STDs.

My boss Sara was a large, enthusiastic British woman in her late forties, who struggled to rule over an office full of temperamental and egotistical men.

'Any tips on how to handle your countrymen, Reetu?' she would say, every now and again, with a hearty laugh.

'You could give all of us lessons, Sara,' I'd counter, with a shudder.

Sara was one of many older single women who headed international health agencies in India. The development sector was flush with others like her—well-qualified women with a voracious, single-minded commitment to their jobs. But despite my admiration for Sara, I couldn't help being put off by her steely, dictatorial manner. Occasionally it struck me that her sharp edge and obsession with her work was related to spending too many years alone, living unchallenged by anyone and without any close relationships. Was I putting myself at risk of becoming this way too? Would I turn into the quintessential shrew?

In many ways, Sara's grit and bossiness was a boon. The workplace was cluttered with several self-important men who did their best to make their presence felt. Fortunately, my job distracted me from their antics. Though my chief role was to manage print media communications about the agency's projects, I was also supposed to advocate on behalf of HIV positive people.

So I made rounds of all the newspaper offices in town in an attempt to influence editors to carry regular features on HIV/AIDS. In the process, I met many bright men, including a Salman Rushdie lookalike, Siddharth Dey, who was also the editor of a popular newspaper.

I saw him for the first time through the glass doors of his office, peering at some newspaper layouts with a colleague, and pointing to sections. He looked up and saw me standing outside. He beckoned for me to enter.

Clearly, Siddharth was prepared for my visit. A mutual friend had set up the meeting, so he greeted me warmly.

'Come, sit, Ritu,' he said, indicating the plush leather sofa on the other side of his office and pressing a buzzer. 'Coffee or tea?' Then he asked me to give him a moment as he turned back to the layout on his desk.

I settled myself into the sofa and picked up a book resting on the glass table beside me. The title on the cover was *Dimming the Lights*, and Siddharth Dey was the author. Before I could turn the page, he came and sat down opposite me. I gave him a quick once-over: he had little round glasses, his beard was well trimmed, but his eyebrows almost met each other, making him look like he was perpetually frowning. He had a bit of a paunch too.

'So how can I help you, Ritu?' he said, looking expectantly at me.

I gave him a spiel about HIV—how it was more widespread than everyone imagined, how much ostracism existed against those who tested positive, and why publications like his should publish stories to inform the public of the situation. When I finished, I handed him a story I'd written on HIV and women. Siddharth skimmed over it expertly.

'Hmm,' he said, 'good copy.'

I was thrilled. 'Thanks, Mr Dey,' I said, trying to conceal my excitement.

'Please call me Sid,' he said, picking up the phone and waving his arm at someone outside. A moment later, a young, bespectacled guy stepped in.

'Dinesh, this is Ritu,' he said, handing him my article. 'Let's carry her story in the Sunday edition.'

When we were alone again, Sid said, 'Look, I can't guarantee that we'll be able to publish too many AIDS-related stories.'

I nodded automatically, too elated by his praise for my story to absorb the full weight of his statement.

Later I learned that Sid was a star journalist, author and editor in the development world, known for his passionate commitment to multiple issues: health, economics, agriculture, global warming and energy conservation. I asked around about him, and wasn't surprised to learn that he was a bachelor, with a large female fan following.

The book I'd picked up was his most recent, an exploration of 'light pollution,' a phenomenon I'd never heard of before. Apparently, the term was coined by astronomers to describe the light that emanated from streetlights, stadiums and other public spaces, and obscured the stars and moon at night.

Sid wrote about how hazardous light pollution was to the health and environment; how it disturbed our body's production of melatonin and led to insomnia; why it confused the flight and migration routes of birds and turned the mating routine of frogs topsy-turvy. Light pollution squandered so much energy, and we were headed for disaster unless action was taken to reduce it.

Sid's fight for the moonlight and starlight fascinated me. Women of my type inevitably develop a massive crush on radical and idealistic men like him, who rely more on their intellect than personal charm quotient to gain attention. Let's face it, highly intellectual and mentally sophisticated men are like magnets. Smart guys can be riveting, despite their narcissism. I found it hard to resist stimulating conversations, and relished the company of men (and women) who held their own.

If they were writers, I fell in love with their words. It

didn't matter whether the guys were old, messy, mean or alcoholic, since I fell for their brains, not their beings. But this was a self-defeating exercise and my attempts to engage romantically with men of the mind have always fallen flat. The thing is, smart guys are arrogant, and generally more concerned with themselves than anyone else. Ideas usually win over relationships for them, which means they aren't the best candidates for a romantic relationship. Even worse is their disregard for women and the casual misogyny that emerges during encounters.

~

My attempts to attract Sid's attention were colourful enough. I did all the stuff the get-your-man books advised: listened to him without interrupting, churned out some of the best writing of my career in a bid to impress him and even carried foil-wrapped slices of my famous chocolate fudge cake every time we had a meeting. I hounded him at book launches and lectures, forcing him to look at me.

Journalism and newspaper offices in those days weren't corporatized as they are today. Conversations and idealism flowed over endless cups of tea and coffee, and I'd drop in on a few editors to discuss possibilities for stories. I added Sid to my list, making my visits seem accidental rather than planned. To my surprise, he always made time for me. On one occasion, he suggested I start a series for his paper, on issues of public health relevance.

'You should think about looking at TB and rare diseases,' he suggested. 'Let's have a drink this evening and talk about it.'

Though I knew my NGO job probably wouldn't allow

me the time to pursue Sid's suggestion, I jumped at the chance to spend time with him.

We met at the press club bar, where he spent most evenings, surrounded by friends, colleagues and his steady flock of admirers. That evening too, he was with two younger men; his voice boomed above theirs, bringing back memories of my biophysics professor in college, Dr D'Souza, whose baritone had all the female students swooning. Sid appeared to have taken on the mannerisms of other, more famous authors: he was bright and articulate but also appeared contemptuous at times, even dismissive of others.

I went up to him tentatively, nodding in greeting at the others.

'Ah here she is, our Ritu,' he said, waving me over. 'Come…come, join us.'

After a round of introductions, the conversation resumed. Talk centered upon his book promotion—his companions were part of his publisher's marketing team.

'It should get to every single college library,' emphasized Sid. 'We need to get young people to start thinking about the hazards of their streetlights.'

There were murmurs of agreement and more talk about the approach they planned to influence the executive boards of educational institutions. I sat back, feeling elated at being a part of this group.

An hour later, we were alone.

'Thanks for supporting my writing,' I said, gazing at him appreciatively. 'I can't tell you how much it means to have my stories published in *News Today*. It's so hard to find editors interested in serious health issues…all they want are articles on super foods and green tea. Every time I try and persuade an editor about the need to have more opinion editorials on health topics like HIV or maternal mortality, they scoff at me. I wonder when everyone will realize that health is as—or more—relevant than politics. A healthy nation is bound to be more productive, and have a higher GDP, obviously...'

Sid downed his drink, looking amused at my speech. He chewed on the ice in his glass contemplatively. 'You sound like an economist! Are you for real? Women like you are a rare breed these days,' he said, sardonically. Confusion flitted across my face. 'Why is that?' I asked, bristling at his use of the word 'breed', and the sarcastic note in his voice. Maybe I was being too touchy: A hypersensitive feminist who protested at every perceived slight?

'Female journalists aren't hard-headed enough to venture into dirty diseases like HIV and TB,' he elaborated. 'They would rather do lifestyle and fashion stories, cover the easy beats that don't need much brainwork.'

I fought the urge to tell him that his views were outdated, and there were enough women journalists around, committed to exploring and reporting on politics, health and other serious issues. The days of women journalists being confined to fashion and 'soft' stories were long since over. How could he, as the head of a newspaper, not know this? I mused about a job I'd once held some years ago, in a newspaper office brimming with men. Edit meetings resembled boys' club gatherings. The women's contributions were mostly ignored, and decision-making was male territory.

Jokes about female body parts were the norm in these

meetings—women above the age of thirty-five were referred to condescendingly as 'aunties' and all senior women editors were expected to participate in the banter. But when it came to story ideas, we were supposed to sit back and let the men decide the important ones. Every single day spent in that office had been a fight for what I considered basic rights.

I recalled the annoyance I felt when a male colleague got to publish his views on the super-bug, which were completely contrary to mine. The editor tossed out my story, and used his instead, ignoring the fact that I was a scientist by training, while the colleague was a BCom. What mattered more was that Mr BCom pass was a male, whose ego would be deeply wounded if his story was pushed out, in favour of mine.

Sitting with Sid evoked the same defensive reaction I'd experienced in that situation. 'Well, I'm absolutely determined to push these issues to the fore… and so is the agency I work for,' I said, tersely.

Sid guffawed. 'You really are delusional, Ritu. I can't imagine how you've allowed yourself to become a part of one of those dubious international agencies led by rich Americans who get huge salaries in the name of helping poor people…What's a nice woman like you towing their line for?' he said derisively.

I was shocked by his arrogance. Blood rushed to my face. I could feel the pounding of my chest, and the weight of my lifelong exhaustion at trying to get men to stop their patronizing banter and treat me like an equal. My disappointment at Sid's true persona silenced me completely.

'You must be hungry,' he said, summoning the waiter. I shrugged when he suggested paneer tikkas. 'Sure, whatever you like.'

He ignored my obvious lack of enthusiasm, and started telling me how tired he was. He said his house was being renovated and he wasn't sleeping well. 'I'm allergic to the smell of the paint,' he said. In addition, his lower back pain had also flared up recently.

'The doctor says it's caused by all the hours I spend at the computer, and travelling,' he told me.

I mentioned an orthopaedic specialist who performed miracles in pain relief, but Sid acted as if he hadn't heard me.

'I'll have to change my lifestyle sooner or later, I know, but how to do this? I am a writer. I am an activist. There's no escaping the computer, or travel...you know my whole life revolves around my causes, they take everything I've got.'

I cut my paneer tikka into two, and wondered whether or not I would be able to maintain my work relationship with Sid, in view of my newly developed antagonism towards him. I reminded myself that he was useful to my career, regardless. Did it really matter that he had revealed himself to be a misogynist and chauvinist?

Sid was on his fifth rum and coke. 'So tell me, Ritu, are you married?' he slurred. I took a deep breath, wondering if it was worth responding. The conversation was unlikely to lead anywhere, especially with the amount of alcohol he had in his system. I'd spent enough time at parties with drunken men, who droned on and on, boring everyone around. Now that my adulation for him had totally evaporated, I couldn't even come up with a ploy to redeem his drunken rambling.

'I was once,' I replied cautiously. 'What about you?'

To my surprise, he exploded in laughter. 'Never!' he guffawed. 'Marriage is the murder of individuality.'

Sid's reaction lightened my mood a little. At least we agreed about something! He made a few more half-hearted attempts to express interest in me, asking me the 'what did you study in college' kind of questions, but his eyes wandered the room when I replied.

I looked around, trying desperately to spot someone, anyone, I knew. Almost miraculously, a friend, Mona, walked in. I stood up and waved at her to come over. Sid greeted Mona as if she was a long-lost friend and asked her about herself. She told him she was a media planner, currently working with a TV network.

'So how do you ladies know each other?' asked Sid, gazing at Mona with undisguised interest.

'We were in the same class at college,' she replied, briskly.

He frowned and gave me a bleary look. 'Really? But Ritu looks older than you. Though she must have been a real beauty in her time,' he said, oblivious to my shocked expression. How did men like him get away with their subtle and not-so-subtle putdowns of women? How could women really fall for their intellectual and liberal personas?

Mona looked at me sympathetically. 'Ready to go?' she said. 'It's really late.'

Sid began protesting, but I had already taken out my wallet and put my share of the bill on the table. 'See you in office sometime, Sid,' I said coolly, taking Mona's arm and moving away.

'I'll call you,' he declared, putting his hand over the notes.

The next day, Sid called while I was in a meeting. Twenty minutes later, he called again. By lunchtime, there were five missed calls from him. Though I had absolutely no desire to talk to him, I steeled myself to dial his number at the end of the day.

'Hi, Sid,' I said cheerily, 'what's happening?'

There was a prolonged silence, and all I could hear was his rapid breath.

'Are you deaf or what?' he snapped. 'Couldn't you hear your phone ringing? I've been calling you all morning.'

I fought the urge to disconnect, reminding myself that there was a professional relationship to maintain.

'Sorry Sid, I've been in meetings all day,' I said, struggling to keep my tone even. 'Was there anything urgent you wanted to discuss?'

'Well, you're a very rude woman, that's for sure,' he said testily, 'for taking so long to call back.'

I sighed. *Here we go again.* By now, I should have been used to the reactions of men who felt slighted by my lack of response to them. After all, a middle-aged woman like me is supposed to respond gratefully when a so-called 'eligible' man makes a move. But I wasn't.

'Listen, I'll be in touch when there's some work to discuss,' I said, putting down the receiver.

12

Bad Boys, Bad Boys What You Gonna Do

Among the pool of single men in the city were a handful of bachelors in their forties and fifties, who fancied themselves as desi James Bonds, based on a grandiose, often delusional self-image. They moved in the fast lane, apparently maintaining a series of casual sexual liaisons. I was told that women gravitated like bees around these rich guys despite their obvious shortcomings: obesity, pomposity, lack of charm and rakish behaviour. Witnessing the modus operandi of one such character was an entertaining experience.

I was introduced to Samir at a friend's fiftieth birthday party. He was short and podgy, about my age, and spoke English with a Hindi enunciation. The ladies flocked around him though. Clearly he had some X factor, which was hard to put a finger on.

'Samir is a topnotch lawyer,' whispered Arti, the hostess. 'Handling the defence in the Pinky Lal case.'

The Pinky Lal case was a high profile tabloid case, in which a rich businessman was suspected of murdering a fashion model, Pinky. The suspicion was that he had pushed her off the balcony of a five-star hotel, though his defence team insisted that the victim had been under the influence of drugs, leading her to leap to her own death.

The knowledge that Samir was defending a rich

murderer made me uncomfortable. I shrugged off the feeling, and picked up a chicken mini-quiche, savouring its flaky pastry. Getting a quiche pastry right was a real art, and I made a mental note to ask Arti who the caterer was.

Bollywood music was on full blast, and the floor was crowded with dancers.

'Come on Ritzy, don't be shy,' shouted someone, pulling my arm and dragging me into the shaking, sweaty mob. I swayed a bit, trying to get into the rhythm. I'd grown up dancing to Boney M and Earth, Wind & Fire, and 'Pappu Can't Dance' kind of music didn't fire up my mojo.

But others seemed to have no problem. Samir lurched towards me, holding the hand of a woman in her twenties, snug in black leather pants.

'Hi Ritu, we met earlier, remember?' he said, rotating his shoulders with abandon. I stepped back and gave him a lukewarm smile.

Now, every woman knows about Indian men and alcohol. A few drinks down, and they start behaving as if the world is their playpen. The drunk Indian male can be spotted from a mile off at parties, clubs and planes. He totters about, slurring his words, making ludicrous statements and leering at every woman who crosses his path. If there's a dance floor around, he's sure to be weaving around, hands in the air, trying to brush his manly chest and every other part of himself against the bodies of females in the vicinity.

Samir looked like he was about to reach that stage. He gyrated aggressively beside me, prompting me to move off the floor, to avoid crashing into him.

'We are going to a nightclub after this, why don't you join us,' he shouted, above the din. 'It'll be good fun.'

I said no quickly, wondering what his game was. Why did a guy who already had a woman hanging onto his arm want a kebab mein haddi? Or did he want a ménage a trios? I didn't stay long enough to find out.

⁓

I ran into Samir again at a book launch, and this time we struck up a conversation about his pro bono work for an NGO working in the field of child rights.

'I have filed five cases for them this year,' he said proudly.

'That's great,' I said, chiding myself for having misjudged him: *Maybe he's not so bad after all.*

I told him about my own work at the Women's and Children's Centre.

'I knew you and I had a lot in common when I saw you, Ritu,' he said, a glint in his eye. 'Let's have a drink soon.' He squeezed my hand before moving away to strike up a conversation elsewhere.

Six weeks later, he sent me a text: *U want to come to the Siddhartha Mukherjee book launch tonight?*

I contemplated his invitation. I was curious about Mukherjee, a US-based physician and oncologist who had authored the Pulitzer Prize-winning book, *The Emperor of All Maladies: A Biography of Cancer.* For the past few years, I'd been a writer for the *Elle* magazine breast cancer campaign, and had a keen interest in learning more about the disease. But at that moment, I was too tired to relish the thought of being crushed in a room with others keen to catch a glimpse of the celebrity writer.

Long day at work, I texted Samir. *Maybe another time.*
How about dinner tomorrow, he countered.

Now, Samir really wasn't my type: he was too plump and self-important. But I decided to be to give him a chance. 'Chuck the checklist,' I recalled some expert say on a dating show. I said yes to his invitation and justified my decision by telling myself that I was just following dating advice. After all, so many friends had told me to be more 'open' to different kinds of men, though I never quite understood what this meant. Open to what? A Sai Baba follower? A taxi driver? A guy ten years younger than me?

Despite my skepticism, I indulged in the fantasy of being swept away by someone completely unlikely. Why not Samir? Hypothetically, he was a good candidate for romance. He was single, my age, professionally successful. So what if he seemed a bit sleazy... or that I had to fight an impulse to correct his pronunciation every time he opened his mouth? What was the harm in checking him out?

We set up to meet the next evening, and Samir arrived to collect me in a chauffeur-driven black BMW. He stepped out of the car to greet me, and opened the door with a flourish. I slid happily into the smooth back seat beside him and murmured, 'Nice.'

He looked pleased. 'Need to maintain my image... being a high-powered lawyer isn't easy,' he said, making a face to indicate the effort involved. 'I have to walk the talk, you know.'

I raised my eyebrows and tried to stifle a laugh. We coasted along to a five-star hotel, and spent a couple of hours downing fish fingers and margaritas. Samir boasted about all the high-profile clients his firm handled: the

Pinky Lal case, and yet another murder trial in which his firm had represented the accused (despite his obvious guilt) and even got him acquitted. I asked him how he felt about letting a murderer loose on society.

'Arre, I would have defended OJ Simpson if he made it worth my while, so why not this guy!' he responded with a laugh.

I was appalled, but decided to give him the benefit of doubt. *Maybe he's just joking?*

Samir went on at length about the cases of fraud, embezzlement and insider trading, which were in the news. We discussed the good-looking girlfriend of a politician he socialized with. The bill arrived. He opened his wallet, and picked out a credit card slowly, making it a point to linger so I could get a look at the dozen cards on display.

When we got back into the car, he squeezed my arm and gave me a suggestive look. 'I've arranged dinner at home,' he said. 'Hope that's okay?'

'That's fine,' I said. *May as well get a close up and see what lies in your bathroom cupboards.* He pressed his thigh against mine, in what seemed to be an appreciative gesture.

'Wait till you see what I've got lined up for you.'

~

My willingness to break the rules of dating and jump ahead to meeting a man in his own house, was more a reflection of my impatience, than my sexual liberation. My logic was: why bother with the fancy dinners if the clues to his personality lie in his living spaces? I was curious about the books people read, the spices in their kitchen and the pictures on their walls.

Samir's flat was located in Jorbagh, one of the most expensive real estate zones of the city. The moment we stepped through the front door, he whipped me off on a tour, beginning with the guest bedroom.

'See—this is an Anjolie Ela Menon,' he said, indicating the giant painting of a Madonna-like figure, wearing a crown of thorns. I murmured appreciatively.

'That's an Arpana Caur, of course,' he boasted, indicating the massive canvas that had a woman holding a pair of scissors as its focus.

'Did you know that Caur uses scissors as a metaphor for time?' he said, 'Based on the Greek belief that scissors can cut a man's fate.'

I made some appreciative sounds, though I wasn't convinced by his speech. Nothing in his demeanour projected the artistic sensibility he was trying so hard to impress me with.

We moved from one room to another, with Samir pointing out the noteworthy objects in each.

'It's a 72-inch screen,' he said, indicating the TV facing his double bed. 'Carried it with me, all the way from Hong Kong so I could watch *Pretty Woman* properly.'

I expelled my breath impatiently: what to say about men and their obsession with giant plasma TVs? Or their fantasies of turning whores into wives? Maybe the latter was more of a possibility, than that of an ugly frog turning into a prince-like husband after all.

My gaze fell to the open suitcase on his bed.

'I'm travelling to Venice tomorrow for a friend's wedding,' he explained, adjusting the suit that lay neatly folded on top. 'All my suits and formal shirts are stitched in Italy, and dry-cleaned only at the Hyatt hotel, you know,' he said, plunging into a long and tedious explanation of where he bought the fabric, how he ensured that he had one case a year in Milan so that he could get his tailoring attended to.

'And here, my assistant maintains my clothes perfectly—they're washed, starched and ironed immediately after use, to avoid stains and smells from accumulating.'

I swallowed a caustic comment, wondering how he would react if I told him that I never dry-cleaned anything, and that I bought most of my clothes at Sarojini Nagar market. Samir's conceit was worth marvelling at, though. I was amused that he imagined that I—or any other woman who wasn't his wife—would be interested in the mundane details of his grooming routine.

Perhaps I should have been impressed at his domestic self-reliance? Obviously, he didn't need a wife to help him maintain his wardrobe. In that sense, he was different from other bachelors I'd met. Maybe his redeeming quality was that he would more likely marry a woman for love, or the value she added to his show-and-tell routine, than to clean up his mess!

~

The showpiece of Samir's study was his iSymphonic Massage chair, a chair that synchronized massage with music.

'Did you know that it was voted "invention of the year" by *Time* magazine,' he said eagerly. 'Come and try it.'

What the hell, I thought, plonking myself on the plush seat. Samir adjusted the settings. 'I've programmed a fifteen-minute neck massage for you,' he said.

The chair started moving to the tempo of *Four Seasons* by Vivaldi. I sat back and mused about Samir's constant references to money. Clearly, he was deprived at some level, and hadn't recovered from this experience. Most of the wealthy guys I knew fell into two categories.

The first were born rich and grew up in an atmosphere of privilege, sent off to Modern School, Doon or Sanawar, followed by college in the UK or US—Oxford, Harvard, Stanford or Yale if they were smart enough. Sure, they threw their weight around, but their comfort around money was apparent. They were even casual about it, since they had never known any kind of material deprivation. From his hints, I gathered that Samir belonged to the second category, those who were born poor or middle-class, and acquired wealth in their adulthood. They were smart and lucky (both generally) to become rich adults.

But they never stopped obsessing about their wealth or pushing their good fortune in other people's faces.

~

Fifteen minutes of the chair massage relieved the tension in my neck. Samir was ready with his next move. He led me to what he referred to as his 'party fridge'. This was packed with wine and chocolates. From the details that peppered his conversation, I gathered that this was part of his courtship ritual. Every woman invited to his apartment was granted access to this fridge.

'Let's have some chardonnay,' he said, pulling out a bottle, 'I just picked it up in Paris.'

I ignored him, transfixed by the chocolates: there were at least ten boxes of Godiva chocolate raspberry truffles, truly the smoothest, melt-in-your mouth chocolates I'd ever eaten in my life. Behind this stash were some giant bars of Cadbury's milk chocolate.

'How come you have Cadbury's,' I exclaimed, 'I thought they were out of fashion.'

My comment pleased Samir. 'Not at all...they are one of my favourite brands...I just love Cadbury's milk chocolate,' he said, pulling out a bar and handing it to me. 'Here's one for you.'

I held the chocolate lovingly, wondering how he would react if I tore the packet open and began eating it. But Samir was too wrapped up in himself to notice my greedy reaction.

'The UK Cadbury's is the best, you know, Ritu,' he said, holding up the chardonnay for my approval.

'I prefer Sula White actually,' I asserted, just to be contrary.

He grimaced and slid the bottle back in the fridge. 'Sab ka apna apna—there's no accounting for personal taste,' he said, carrying the Sula and two wine glasses into the drawing room.

We sat down on the white sofa, and after some banter about our work, the conversation moved to relationships. I asked him about the woman he was with at the party.

He laughed dismissively. 'Oh her...she's the daughter of a high court judge. I was just entertaining her since she was in town that day.'

I then asked him whether there was any truth in the rumour that he was involved with a mutual friend of ours—I didn't want to get caught in the middle of anything.

'How could you even imagine me with *her*, Ritu?' he said, in a pained voice. 'I only go out with good-looking women.'

I gulped my wine, taken aback by his chauvinism, and this negative judgment of our friend. So, her looks didn't meet his standards. What a creep. Had he actually looked at himself in the mirror properly?

'Actually I have a gorgeous girlfriend in Venice,' he said quickly, seeing that I was put out.

A bearer brought in a plate of chicken tikkas, and I was distracted. I took a bite of the succulent morsel on my plate and savoured it, in an attempt to regain my composure.

'Oh really…so the long-distance relationship thing works for you then?' I ventured.

'Oh come on, Ritu, there are trains and planes! We get together whenever we can,' he began. 'The rest of the time we are free to pursue other options…it's an open relationship…there are so many beautiful women out there…'

My distaste built up. His 'I'm the greatest guy in the universe' stance was like a wall he'd built to support himself. And adulation was his biggest craving, so when it came to women, Samir was on the lookout for ladies to fan his narcissism. In return, he was ready to open his wallet. Even though he was ageing and not particularly attractive, his wealth ensured him a steady supply of women agreeable to this arrangement.

'I'm glad you've got it all sorted out, Samir,' I said, in an even tone.

He refilled my wine glass and moved close to me. His hand reached out for my knee. 'You are a sexy woman,

Ritu, and I'd love to spend more time with you,' he murmured. 'And you can trust me—my lips will be sealed.'

I took his hand off my knee, and excused myself to go to the bathroom. I stared at my reflection in the mirror: dishevelled, flushed, from the wine and irritation, and definitely tired. Why had I put myself through the whole wine-and-dine routine with a guy like him, who bribed me with a session in his massage chair and a bar of imported chocolate, to induce me into his bed?

Of course, it was my fault. I'd agreed to have dinner at his house and he'd imagined that my apparently progressive attitude meant I was up for casual sex. How was he to know that his bed-hopping ethos was as off-putting to me as his bragging? Or that his offer to maintain secrecy about our sex life—if we ever had one—was probably the worst move he could have ever made. Men like him made sex dirty, I mused, tearing open the bar of Cadbury's and popping a large chunk into my mouth. By the time I walked out of the bathroom, I was clear about one thing: if a guy looks sleazy, he is sleazy.

∼

I'd heard some stories about the bad boys of Delhi, who charmed the panties off women and disappeared soon thereafter. Their role models were Hollywood heroes like Jude Law and Colin Farrell, whose rakish charm was reputed to drive females mad. Though women instinctively knew that they wouldn't get a lasting relationship out of them, very few had the willpower to resist them. Hymens and hearts were broken as these charming and commitment-phobic men moved from one woman to the next.

None of the men I met even remotely resembled Jude Law, so I didn't believe the rumours. 'Maybe people refer to sleazy characters as bad boys here,' I remarked, to my friend Poonam, while we sipped happy hour cocktails at TGIF.

'Maybe,' she said, 'but we do tend to fall for the wicked guys... maybe because we know we can't ever *have* them, you know.'

We were on our fourth glass of Long Island iced tea, and Poonam was swirling on her bar stool a bit too vigorously. 'Let's accept that we are total suckers for men who take us for a spin,' she giggled.

I laughed disbelievingly. The thought of falling for a commitment-phobic party boy was ludicrous. Why waste time playing dead-end seduction games with anyone? I couldn't imagine being a plaything for any man.

My confidence in my capacity to automatically reject anyone with bad boy characteristics didn't prepare me for my first encounter with one. I met Mukesh through an ex-colleague, Ravi, at a wedding reception. Ravi introduced him as a 'chum from school', and started telling him about me, recounting the time we worked together on an NGO project in the red-light district of Mumbai. Our job was to persuade sex workers to enroll their children in school.

Mukesh's eyes lit up with interest at Ravi's description of the brothels we visited. 'What was that like?' he asked me curiously.

'A bit dismal,' I said, feeling a little ashamed about this admission. 'The place was a giant slum and the rooms were like hovels... and the women conducted their business while the kids played outside.'

Mukesh moved closer to me and gave me one of those appraising looks, which started from my hair and eyes, paused at my breasts, before flicking downwards and ending at my toes. I shifted my weight from one foot to the other. The gaze of the male hunter seemed outdated, so I decided to get even by subjecting him to the same assessment. Mukesh had a dusky complexion, high cheekbones, and gelled hair. He wore a slick navy blue suit, with a mauve tie, which reminded me of Robert de Niro in *Casino*. He was good-looking in an Italian mobster kind of way too.

Both of us reached out for a glass of red wine when the waiter made his rounds with the drinks tray.

'Aha,' said Mukesh, giving me another appraising look, 'so we do have something in common after all!'

Ravi raised his glass of whisky, and we followed suit. 'Cheers!'

'Is wine a dancer's drink or what?' Ravi asked Mukesh mock-seriously.

'Probably,' replied Mukesh, 'since it's the only alcoholic beverage you can drink without worrying about losing your balance.'

'Really?' I retorted. 'So how many glasses can you drink without feeling tizzy?'

'Two… three maybe,' he responded. 'What about you?'

'Wine isn't really my drink,' I said. 'I'd rather have a chilled beer.'

Mukesh made a face and put down his empty glass on a nearby table. 'So why didn't you have beer today?' He gestured to the waiter for another round.

'I've got some work to finish when I get home,' I said, sipping my drink slowly, 'and beer makes me sleepy.'

Ravi nodded in agreement. 'Remember the beer promotion event we went to?' he said. We launched into another nostalgic chat about past lives.

'So Ritu, what do you do over the weekend?' quizzed Mukesh, cutting into our exchange.

'A bit of this and that,' I replied, wondering which of my interests I should talk about. Reading? Baking? Watching movies? Working out?

It was easier to throw the question back at him. 'What do you do on holidays, Mukesh?'

'I spend all my free time in my dance studio,' he said. 'Latin dance is my thing. Can you do salsa or zumba?'

Ravi's dig at him about wine being a dancer's drink now began to make sense, but I wondered whether he was serious: did I look like a zumba or salsa dancer?

'Oh no,' I replied quickly. 'I love music but I really can't do any dance except disco-style shaky wiggly stuff. I've absolutely no sense of co-ordination.'

Mukesh raised his eyebrows in amusement at my statement.

'Shaky wiggly stuff...that sounds exciting. But I can teach you salsa if you want,' he murmured.

I kept silent, not sure how to respond: why would I want to learn dance from Mukesh, or anyone for that matter?

'Do get in touch if you're interested,' he said, unperturbed by my discomfort. He handed me a blue business card from his wallet. Mukesh Rastogi, it read. Below his name was a long list of qualifications. The MBA from Wharton caught my eye.

'I work in the family business of stock market advisory,

with my dad,' he explained, mentioning an address in Connaught Place.

My interest was piqued. How often did one meet a guy with an MBA who was an expert salsa dancer too? Most guys I knew were relatively unidirectional. They were boxed into their careers and identities. Mukesh appeared to have chucked the standard formula and devised his own, more innovative one. I put his card in my handbag and gave him one of my own.

'I'll give you a call,' he said, his gaze skittering across the room. A moment later, he was gone. I looked at Ravi questioningly. 'Who is this guy?'

Ravi gave me a quizzical smile. 'He's good company and a great dancer—that much I know, but don't get too cozy with him. I've been told he's a big ditcher when it comes to women.'

~

The thought of Mukesh crossed my mind a few times after our encounter, and I wasn't surprised when he called. 'So pretty lady, how's it going?' he said breezily.

I told him about an article I was planning, on dance therapy, and asked if he would introduce me to his clients who could talk about the physical and emotional benefits of dance. He responded enthusiastically. 'That's fantastic. I'm going to put you in touch with some people in my class.'

I thanked him, feeling strangely gratified about having found some way of connecting with him. I needn't have worried though, since he had worked out his own route. 'Listen, I'm calling to invite you to my birthday party,' he continued.

I smiled at the excitement in his voice; it was rare to meet a guy in his forties who made a big deal of his birthday. 'I'd love to come,' I replied. 'Please text me the address.'

The party venue was a farmhouse on the outskirts of the city. There were lots of cars with CD plates. Little fairy lights twinkled on the trees, and from the gate, I could see the large gathering of guests at the far corner of the sprawling garden. Strains of Latin music filled the air, and I was instantly lifted by the atmosphere of festivity.

I spotted some well-known artists, designers and business magnates, lots of glamorous women and some Western men. Waiters wandered around serving vol-au-vents and stuffed mushrooms, and Mukesh stood in the midst of a group of women, dressed in a tight black suit.

'Hey, glad you could make it,' he said, giving me a European-style peck on both cheeks and taking my gift of red wine from my hands. 'Let me introduce you to my friends.'

An hour later, I moved with the crowd to a dance floor set in a courtyard, below the trees. Couples shimmied away to the rhythm of a salsa song, 'Oye Como Va', being belted out by Celia Cruz. I mused about how much better I liked Santana's version, and gazed enviously at the floor full of dancing people.

My attempts to learn formal dance of any kind had never met with much success. I never seemed to get the steps right and partnering with a man on the dance floor didn't come easy either. Every time I did one of those couple numbers, I'd tug at my partner and frustrate him.

I just couldn't let anyone take the lead. I thought about my ineptitude as I watched Mukesh dancing with a slim olive-skinned woman in a short black skirt and heels that looked like killers. They were a joy to watch together: Mukesh moved his torso and shoulders smoothly in sync with the drumbeat, and led his partner with the same ease. In a flash, I could see what made him so attractive to women. His agility and easy reading of his partner's rhythm were sure bait.

I came away from the party with mixed feelings. My attraction to Mukesh had intensified, but I also felt insecure. What was the point of even considering starting up something with him? He was so different from me: so smooth, flamboyant and easy in his body. How could I—a middle-aged, not-so-thin woman with zero grace on the dance floor—possibly match up to the young, agile women he danced with every day? What were the chances of my assimilating into his world of dance and music?

And how would he fit into my world? I wondered whether he'd be able to contribute to a conversation about health systems, or medicine. With a sigh, I realized that the chances of coupling successfully with a man like him were almost nil.

~

Still, I couldn't curb my elation when he called to invite me to accompany him to a dinner party. 'It's at a good friend's place…he's a great host.' I accepted his invitation, not pausing for an instant to worry about the risks of accompanying a man I barely knew, to a stranger's house.

Mukesh began describing how he and Bobby used to be best pals at school. 'Now his wife and her friends come to my dance studio, can you imagine!' he said.

I laughed, despite my uncertain feelings. Every woman in his circle was either a dancer, or on her way to becoming one. The only way to belong was to follow suit.

'Any dress code?' I asked, tentatively.

'Wear something revealing,' he responded, with a guffaw. I was taken aback. Was he serious? I recalled the beautiful women at his party, with their bare-backed dresses and plunging necklines. Nothing in my wardrobe came even close to glamorous, let alone revealing.

He sensed my hesitation, and was quick to cover up. 'Just kidding. You look great in everything.'

I took hours trying to decide what to wear, trying out unworn blouses and skirts from the piles at the back of my cupboard and peering at my reflection in a mirror. I would never have the lithe body of the female dancers he was used to. I convinced myself to wear a pink blouse that clung to me anyway, and a vivid five-panelled skirt designed by my friend Komal.

From under the bed, I pulled out a pair of purple spangled sandals that had been lying in a shoebox since I bought them a year earlier. I tottered around in them, recalling my excitement when I first saw them, in the shop of a Chinese shoemaker. 'When will you ever wear four-inch heels?' chided my sister, in an attempt to dissuade me from buying them. I mused about sending her a picture.

Mukesh made lots of admiring noises when he picked me up. 'You're looking really hot,' he said, giving me his signature top-to-toe look, as I slid into the front seat of his car. 'Pink suits you.'

I flushed at his obvious appreciation, and fought back my amusement: wasn't the word 'hot' best applied to someone half my age? But then, Mukesh was a 45-year-old who acted as if he was twenty-five. He even lived the life of a much younger man.

We drove along in Saturday night traffic. The dinner party was in Gurgaon, so there was a long way to go. To my surprise, he turned on some opera, and began humming along with Pavarotti. The leather interiors of the car throbbed with the emotion, and my heart leapt.

'I'm learning to sing opera myself, at the Italian embassy, twice a week,' he divulged.

'That's wonderful,' I murmured, marvelling at whatever force on the planet had placed me in a car with a salsa dancer and self-proclaimed opera singer, after months of hanging around with a slew of dull men.

'You know dance and music has changed my whole life,' he said reflectively. 'I was a complete nonentity at one time.'

'That's hard to imagine, Mukesh,' I said, struggling to summon an image of him as a nondescript everyday man, who went about business as usual.

I also bit back my urge to tell him how stunning he was on the dance floor—all the dating guides I'd read stressed holding back feelings, and prolonging a man's uncertainty.

'I never got a second look from anyone when I was in college,' he continued. 'And none of the girls wanted to go out with me.'

He said he'd started learning dance as part of a personality enhancing exercise. 'I knew I wasn't smart enough to become a rich man and lure the girls with my money,' he said. 'So I bought some dance tapes and began practicing in my bedroom...who knew that I'd be running a dance studio twenty years later!'

'You're lucky to have found your calling,' I said. My thoughts strayed to some people I knew, who'd been stuck in dead-end jobs and marriages all their lives, and never had the courage to follow their passion. Timing really mattered, and Mukesh's success in capitalizing upon his passion for dancing had much to do with the fact that he'd taken this up early, when he was young and energetic enough to chase whatever he wanted.

'Yes, but what to do about the wine-drinking?' he said playfully. 'You tell me, you're the health expert.'

Apparently Mukesh had just recovered from a hepatic infection. 'I spent a month in hospital, and the doc said I needed to cut back on the booze, long-term.'

The image of his vulnerable liver loomed in my head, and I could feel my protective instinct coming to the fore. I searched my brain for whatever I could summon up about liver health.

'That's bad—but there's no choice—recovering liver health is a long process. You'll need to avoid booze, fried foods, too much exertion,' I cautioned. 'You must eat a bowl of dahi every day.'

He nodded, looking bored and simultaneously worried. 'I'm trying. But you know wine and dance go together… sometimes I lose track of how much goes down,' he sighed.

I started to speak again, and stopped, reminding myself of one particular session with AD years earlier, in which she'd said: *Stop trying to mother, advise and fix every man you meet*. Indeed, playing Mother Teresa had failed me in the department of love: how easily stories of let-down and despair triggered my self-sacrificial tendencies. I decided I would be ultra careful about keeping this particular tendency of mine under control, this time round.

I gave Mukesh an affectionate pat on his knee instead, and he closed his hand over mine, giving it a squeeze. I left it there for an instant, letting the surge of warmth from his touch course though my fingers.

But Mukesh broke the spell. 'I need to pick up some flowers,' he said, veering off the highway, and stopping near a flower vendor. He turned to me beseechingly. 'Could you help me choose? I don't know anything about flowers.'

～

The party was in full swing when we walked in. The host, Bobby, and his wife Safina greeted Mukesh effusively. They tried to look impressed when Mukesh introduced me.

'Ritu is a big-time journalist who writes for all kinds of papers and magazines.'

Safina's attention had already wandered to another couple who had just entered the room. 'Excuse me,' she said, traipsing off in her chiffon saree.

I moved my weight from one foot to the other, trying to distract myself from my discomfort as I looked around and realized I had chosen the wrong clothes for the occasion.

My tight blouse and billowing skirt were totally inappropriate, since all the other women were clad in sarees or salwaar kameezes. Why hadn't Mukesh warned me? I glared at him balefully.

'Let me get you a beer,' he said, gently steering me towards the bar. He greeted several people on the way, shaking hands with the men and exchanging plenty of air-kisses with the women. 'She takes my classes,' he'd say, indicating one woman or another. I nodded each time, astonished that salsa was such a popular form of dance in Delhi.

The hostess suddenly appeared before me, and took me to a group of women. 'This is Ritu—Mukesh's *friend*,' she said, emphasizing the last word and giving me a knowing look and wink. I started opening my mouth to protest, but stopped. What was the point? I had already been branded.

Yet again, my tendency to overlook the implications of my actions in the arena of relationships, or worry about how they could be misread, was my undoing. Self-recrimination flooded through me, until Mukesh reappeared to distract me. His hand skimmed the small of my back, before he started greeting the others in the circle. I envied the ease with which he stepped in and out of the female orbit, which contrasted so sharply with my own awkwardness.

My wariness with married women in social situations tinged my interactions. Finding common ground hadn't been easy since I'd become a singleton. Their conversations revolved around husbands, children, in-laws, maids, vacations and shopping trips. I had nothing to contribute; my concerns were different, as were my victories: discovering a great plumber, paying rent on time, and publishing an article in a paper with a wide circulation. I wondered what they'd make of my mission to find Mr Right.

'So what do you do?' ventured someone bravely.

'I'm a health writer,' I replied, trying to sum up my entire existence in one sentence. Fortunately, this elicited lots of chatter about diets and weight problems, and I relaxed as the evening progressed. Mukesh hovered around, never letting me feel abandoned.

He seemed to have his finger on my pulse, sensing when I was restless or hungry, or simply needed rescuing from a conversation. He watched my glass, refilling it whenever it fell empty and kept bringing around the bowls of nuts and chips.

The rest of the evening was spent in a haze of pheromones. Everything he said or did simply worked to build up the fantasy I had created about him. He picked up on my vibe, bestowing me with all the attention and alcohol I could possibly want. Two hours later, I was wilting. 'I'm really tired,' I moaned, grabbing his arm.

'That's because you haven't had the right drink,' he purred, 'I'm going to make you a special one.' Despite my protests, he walked away to the bar and came back bearing a glass filled with a red drink. I reeled after my first sip. 'It's heady, just like you,' he said, stroking my arm. 'I can't wait for it to hit you.'

Before I could respond, a group of women waved to him, and he responded by summoning them over. There was plenty of laughter, and a round of introductions. While Mukesh basked in their attention, I abandoned my drink on a nearby tray. Ten minutes later, I pulled at his arm. 'Let's go, please, it's really late.' This time, Mukesh knew by my tone that I meant business.

~

We got into the car in silence. Mukesh opened the glove compartment to retrieve the glasses he used for driving at night. 'Where the hell are they,' he muttered, rummaging around noisily. Something fell on my feet. We bent down to pick up the packet simultaneously. I froze when I saw the box of Masti condoms resting against my silvery purple sandals. Mukesh picked it up nonchalantly and put it back in the compartment. 'Now you know I practice safe sex, right?'

When Mukesh dropped me home an hour later, I was tempted to invite him in. But I decided against it, and wished him goodnight with a peck on his cheek. Despite my attraction to him, I wasn't ready for a physical relationship.

Even if I took the plunge, I wasn't sure about my readiness to handle the repercussions. Would I fall into the familiar trap, the blame game I'd witnessed so many progressive and liberated women playing? *He lured me into bed... He used me...*

I recalled conversations with outwardly bold and brazen women who pretended to be sexually liberated, but couldn't resist accusing men of 'taking advantage' of them when copulation didn't lead to the commitment they sought.

There was M, an ex-colleague who had all the men lusting for her, with her plunging necklines and skimpy skirts. She used the F word in every sentence and was open about her affairs with various men, including her bosses. Known for getting entangled with 'unavailable men,' M believed it was perfectly acceptable to have sex with guys on the first date. She hounded them thereafter, calling them up a dozen times a day to suggest more dates, and was heartbroken when the men didn't return her calls.

Once, she and I got into a heated discussion over whether society had the right to blame men for the suicide of women they'd jilted. The sensational story of a failed love affair that had led a supermodel to jump to death had just broken. The 23-year-old had left a note blaming her boyfriend for failing to deliver on his promise of marriage.

'What a bastard... any man who promises a woman he will marry her and doesn't, after sleeping with her, should be jailed for life,' M ranted, taking a deep suck of her cigarette.

I sipped the watery coffee from the office machine and wondered if she was saying this for dramatic effect. But M was dead serious. Her forward sexual behaviour conflicted with the meaning she attributed to sex, and I suddenly realized that her swaggering bravado was just a cover up for her vulnerability.

'How dare these guys assume they can f...k whoever they want and get away with it.'

Linking sex to love is one matter, but tying it up with marriage was ludicrous. I tried to reason with her.

'What about sexual freedom? How can we be at par with men we sleep with, unless we exercise the same choice as them... attribute as little or as much meaning to the sexual act as they do?' M gave me a dirty look, threw her cigarette to the floor, and crushed it with her heel.

From this conversation, I realized that easy sex isn't as easy as it looks, even for bold women who fight against gender stereotypes and take pride in 'living like men.' Claiming sexual power was nearly impossible for my friend Avantika, who had plenty of other masculine traits she enjoyed boasting about. She had walked out of a bad marriage without a second thought, and successfully negotiated big business deals. But she just couldn't handle a sexual relationship that came without strings.

Ironically, Avantika was an Oshoite and used her guru's philosophies of love to justify her clandestine relationships with married or otherwise unavailable men. *Marriage is meaningless… love doesn't need social sanction… we are free to love whoever falls on our path.*

But Osho's views on sexual freedom were completely wasted on her. The moment she had sex with a guy, she became insecure and began seeking constant reassurance. She demanded that he love her fully—like a wife—and lost any negotiating power she may have had, right at the start. Her lovers were frightened of her intensity, and backed off the moment they could. Avantika's desperation mounted. 'The asshole said he was too busy supervising his son's studies to meet me, can you believe it?' or 'The bugger said his wife needs him more than I do,' and so on. All her talk of detachment evaporated into thin air, and she ended up hounding the guys till they changed their telephone numbers or moved away.

~

Despite the feeling that I was playing with fire, I couldn't control my euphoria at Mukesh's text, the morning after the party: *GM Hot Lady. Thanks for a great night.*

I called my friend Poonam and told her the whole story.

'He sounds familiar,' she countered. 'I hope it's not the same guy another friend was telling me about—he was also a salsa dancer, a real player.'

'Must be someone else,' I said briskly, ignoring the racing of my pulse at the thought of Mukesh with other women. One part of me knew that a man like him was likely to play the field, but another tiny voice told me he was my man. He was like a drug that held out the promise of a quick high. But I was supremely confident that I wouldn't get hooked.

So far, no substance or person in my existence had made me abandon myself. What was the harm in riding the wave of attraction and letting things play out? Maybe he would make me change my mind about love and life.

When Poonam called later to report that Mukesh was indeed the same guy who had broken many women's hearts, I told her not to worry about me.

'I can take care of myself,' I insisted.

∼

The next time we met, Mukesh shared his big heartbreak story with me; the one about *that* life-changing, soul-crushing love affair that didn't end like a fairytale. 'Marika was Spanish, on a visit to India,' he said.

'We were in our twenties and I was so crazy about her that I moved to Spain to be with her.' They had a dramatic relationship that consisted of daily shouting matches and amazing make-up sex. 'The passion and anger was addictive,' he confessed.

When the inevitable breakup happened, he packed his bags and returned to India. 'I was devastated.'

Despite his attempts to maintain steady, regular relationships with women, the humdrum of daily interaction bored him quickly. 'I keep trying to recreate the high I had with Marika,' he said ruefully.

Though I was discomfited by the fact that a meaningful romantic relationship was off his agenda, I felt a rush of warmth for what I convinced myself was honesty—the intimate disclosure was a measure of his trust in me, and made me feel closer to him. Also, the lure of sexual fulfillment was hard to ignore. Maybe I hoped that being with him would help me loosen up, perhaps even adopt a more flexible view to casual sex, within the context of a loose romantic relationship.

But the opportunity to take things further with Mukesh never arose. He disappeared, just as quickly as he'd appeared. I waited to hear from him, but he didn't call. I dialled his number a few times, but our conversations were always vague. When I suggested meeting up, he made excuses: *In the middle of practice for a big event right now... Just leaving for my niece's wedding in Pune... Laid up with the 'flu.*

I struggled with feelings of rejection and a crushing awareness of my own stupidity: *How could you be so delusional... Everyone told you about him... What's wrong with you...?* The disparity between his world and mine was obvious, and I wondered why I'd imagined they could ever merge.

The stories I told myself about Mukesh's change of heart varied though, depending on my mood. I told Poonam that I regretted playing hard to get; that I should have been more brazen about my willingness to get intimate with him, in time. But the true story was the hardest to tell: that Mukesh was used to dancing his way quickly into women's beds; that he didn't like to wait; and that he wasn't interested in a relationship with me. For men like him, love was only about the chase. Once they got to the finish line, things were over.

13
Metamorphosis into a Desi Cougar

My decision to join the gym was driven by the glimpse I caught of my expanding backside in one of those mall department stores with multiple mirrors. I noticed my stomach was jutting too, and dialled my mother immediately. 'Am I looking fat?' I asked sorrowfully.

My mother laughed. 'Don't worry—I've put on weight too,' she said comfortingly.

My friend circle had advised me to join a gym long before this fatty moment, on the basis that it was the best place to meet new people. 'You must expand your social circle,' nagged a married pal, who had spent every evening for the past twenty years hanging out in front of her TV with her husband.

I had ignored her advice, since the idea of communal exercise had never appealed: what a group of sweating, breathless people derived from hanging around together was a mystery to me. My idea of exercise was a walk in the park and a few stomach crunches in front of the TV. But my expanding girth clearly called for more vigorous measures.

Gyms were a hotbed of affairs, from what I'd heard. One of my newspaper colleagues, Ruma, had run away with her trainer. This incident shocked me, because Ruma had always made so much of her blissful, romantic marriage.

Every Thursday she and her spouse had a dinner date, and she made it a point to announce her plans to the whole office.

Whenever someone suggested an official get together on that day, Ruma protested vehemently. 'No way folks, how can you expect me to cancel my candlelight dinner with my husband—you know how much it means,' she'd say, with a wink.

One day, she didn't show up for work. A week later, she was still missing. Her boss complained that she hadn't taken either sick or casual leave and announced he was going to cut her pay.

We knew something was wrong when the police showed up and interrogated us: had any of us heard from Ruma in the last week? Had she discussed her gym trainer, Manoj, with us? Did we know she was unhappy in her marriage? None of us were prepared for the news that she had run away with the trainer, leaving her husband a farewell note that informed him that the divorce papers were en route.

Another much-talked about romance that began in a gym was between Jane, the 51-year-old director of an international development agency, and Roland, her 35-year-old trainer. Apart from the age difference, the disparity in their social backgrounds and educational levels added spice to the gossip about their relationship: Roland was a 'BA pass' from Kurukshetra University in Haryana, while Jane held a doctorate in health communications from Johns Hopkins University in Baltimore, USA.

Her friends and colleagues made mean jokes about Roland's rustic manner and lack of intellect behind her back. 'It's really hard to keep the conversation going when he's around,' said one, 'He doesn't read or have an opinion about politics or anything.' But Jane paid no heed to the gossip, and continued to take Roland to dinner parties. Last I heard, they had moved to Washington D.C. together.

So, it was with trepidation that I joined Bodylicious, a small and plush neighbourhood gym that had a cafeteria with the best banana smoothies I've ever tasted. Every morning I donned a baggy t-shirt and track pants and spent an hour sweating it out between the treadmill and free-style body-weight training—push-ups, crunches and squats.

It was agony. I barely noticed the other men and women around, since my personal quest to get into shape was so overwhelming. The trainers were kind and helpful; they didn't seem like the sorts who would run off with women, but then who knew?

I usually ended my routine with a steam and sauna, and chatted with other women while I soaked up the steam. Everyone enjoyed handing out advice on health, weight, fashion and skin therapies. So I didn't mind when some ladies suggested I needed a new look.

'You've lost some weight so why not show it off with sexier clothes,' said Sanya, a tall woman in her thirties who ran at high speed on the treadmill. 'And some exercise bras too.'

We went shopping that afternoon. And the next day, I entered the gym self-consciously, feeling like a stuffed chicken in my new workout bra and blue lycra exercise pants.

'You'll get used to it,' said Sanya dismissively, when I complained about my discomfort. A few minutes into my workout, I realized I was eliciting a lot more attention than usual.

In the mirror, I spotted a lean, tall man a few feet away, who kept glancing my way. He had the chiselled looks and muscular torso of a model. I gave him a sidelong glance, and he was quick to pick up on my interest. After a few days of skirting around and darting flirtatious looks at each other, he came up to me.

'I'm Vijay,' he said.

After I had introduced myself, he asked me what I did for a living.

'I'm a journalist… writer, sort of both,' I said, confused as usual about how to define my occupation.

'Well, I'm into carpets,' he stated. I pushed away the image of him bare-chested and encased in a Kashmiri silk rug, and tried to focus on what he was saying.

'I own a carpet export business,' he said.

'Oh great… maybe you can advise me on where to pick up a good rug,' I said. 'I've been looking for one of those thick and silky kinds, but I haven't found anything I like in the market.'

'Don't worry, you'll get your dream rug from me.' He smiled and handed me his business card. 'Give me a call any time.'

I whipped out my card too, and thrust it into his hand.

After this encounter, I began pondering about Vijay's age. Was he five years younger than me or ten? I discussed the situation with my group of advisors.

'Stop worrying about it,' said Sanya. 'You're not planning to marry him or anything, are you?'

The pairing of middle-aged women with much younger men was a mystery to me, till then, despite the glamourizing of this union by Madonna, Courtney Cox and Demi Moore. Referred to as 'cougars' in popular culture, older women who gravitate towards younger men are believed to be in their sexual element.

Also known as the puma or mountain lion, the cougar pursues a wide variety of prey, ranging from cattle to tiny insects. Women compared to cougars are believed to be predatory and have a sexuality that is 'deviant' and 'bestial', reflecting the disregard they have for the rigid rules that define female sexual behaviour. The growing presence of cougars in society apparently threatens the mating behaviour of men.

Theories about what drives women to becoming cougars varied: one was that women above the age of thirty-five are prompted by their shrinking ovaries, to go out on a desperate sexual rampage. Since their baby-making days are limited, they are anxious to jump into bed with just about anyone. Another theory is that the sexual drive of an older woman was more closely matched to that of a younger man, than someone of her own age.

My own take was more boring. I believed that older women gravitated towards younger men for more banal reasons such as the shortage of single, interesting men of their own age. Younger men, in comparison, were available in large numbers, easy to befriend, had less baggage and fewer hang-ups. And they were also fitter.

One of the most off-putting things about some Indian guys above the age of forty is their poor physical shape. It's hard to find a reasonably healthy-looking, middle-aged male—a guy whose flesh isn't spilling out over his belt. Though some pals advised me to stop worrying about looks and focus on 'the beauty inside', I simply wasn't able to overlook the flab.

To me, the disregard of guys for their bodies reflected their indolence and lackadaisical attitude to health in general. How to consider a relationship with someone so careless about his physical well-being? If a man can't walk up a flight of steps without panting, what kind of companion would he make for woman who enjoyed swimming, running and travelling? Surely this was valid enough reason for women to strike up relationships with younger men who were more their equal in the pool?

This was a reasonable enough theory, especially since I wasn't convinced that romantic relationships thrived only when women were younger than their partners. In my view, the age difference between a romantically involved man and woman was inconsequential, when marriage wasn't on the agenda.

~

A week after we'd exchanged numbers, Vijay called to invite me for dinner at Mainland China. An hour before we were supposed to meet, he called again to request a change in plans. 'Listen, I'm running a slight fever,' he said. 'Why don't you come over to my place instead?'

I was unsure how to react: though I'd broken the rule of 'never go to a man's house on your first date', this was different, since I knew absolutely nothing about Vijay.

I called Sanya for advice. 'Things are different now,' she said authoritatively. 'Women drop in on guys all the time…I'll call you to check on you, promise.'

I contemplated what she'd said, and decided it was just too bad if Vijay got the 'wrong' idea about me.

I told Vijay I'd come over for a short while.

'But I'm carrying chilli powder in my handbag,' I said half-seriously.

He snorted in response. 'Don't worry—you can use my gun.'

~

His apartment was on the second floor of a building in a neighbourhood close by. But there was no light in the stairwell, and I panicked while stumbling up the stairs in the dark. *What am I doing here? What if he's a psycho? Oh God...*

But there was no time to retract, since the door upstairs swung open before I got there.

'Heard you coming up,' said Vijay. He was clad in a tatty vest and pair of shorts.

I was taken aback, then reminded myself that he wasn't well (or so he'd said). Still, I couldn't hold back the disappointment: *where's the stud from the gym gone?*

I had donned my favourite boots and a Zara suede jacket for the occasion and Vijay's dishevelled appearance made me feel foolish and overdressed.

'Wow, you've very fashionable,' he said, putting his arm around my shoulders, and leading me to the maroon leather sofa. 'How is it that you aren't married, a woman as hot-looking as you?'

I shrugged, not sure what he wanted to hear. How did guys get away with asking this question, in this day and age?

'I was married once,' I said with some trepidation. This line had silenced others before him, and I knew it would shut him up quickly, unless he was interested in listening to the saga of a marital breakup.

But Vijay was too occupied with his seduction game to pay attention to what I said. The low-hanging lights in his sitting room cast a pinkish hue over everything, reminding me of bordellos in the movies, and a car I'd travelled in recently. The backseat of this famous Ambassador (which was named Basanti by its owner, my friend Julian) had been remodelled into a gold and pink sofa. Silvery cushions and baubles that dangled from the roof cast a rosy glow like the one in Vijay's room, over its passengers. The fame of Basanti spread far and wide, and she had even been featured in a Bollywood film.

I mused about how the lighting in Vijay's living room was sleazy in comparison. A mattress covered with a white sheet was strategically set on the other side of the room. *Kaun Banega Crorepati* Season Two was on. Two crore rupees was on the line. Amitabh Bachchan's booming voice resonated off the walls.

'Beer okay?' asked Vijay, bringing out two bottles of Kingfisher Extra Strong from the fridge. 'Sorry this was the only brand around,' he explained, seeing my dismayed expression.

'Oh well,' I said stoically, 'guess it'll have to do.'

Isn't serving a woman Kingfisher Extra Strong equal to putting Ecstasy in her drink? I pacified myself with the thought that a guy who was upfront about his intentions to get a woman lose her balance was better than one who was sly about it.

I walked around the room, sipping the foul-tasting brew and peering at the pictures on the wall. One side of the room was dominated by a series of framed photos. These were all of Vijay: posing in a suit, lined up on a stage with four other men, shaking hands with Shah Rukh Khan, taking a trophy from the hands of some big-shot industrialist.

'When were these taken?' I asked.

'During my modelling days five years ago,' he said. 'I was second in the Mr India contest, you know.'

Vijay started telling me what a charmer the actor had been during the awards ceremony, how he got a contract with Versace soon afterwards, and another one with Christian Dior a year later. I made some admiring noises, imagining the stir the story of my evening with Mr Top Model would create at the female sauna gathering.

'So what was it like being a model?'

'Rough business,' he said, warming to the subject. 'Meant working out like crazy to keep in shape, spending days and nights at photo shoots, travelling every week, dealing with mean people...' When he turned thirty-four, he realized his modelling days were numbered, and decided to turn to carpet exports instead. Since then, he had worked twelve-hour days to get the business running.

'Really? What about family and social life?' I asked, curiously.

'Family means nothing, kuch matlab nahi,' he shrugged. 'Parents are in Mumbai and I haven't seen them for a decade.'

He flicked channels as he talked, settling on a movie with Shilpa Shetty. 'Work and gym is all that counts,' he declared, pulling out a catalogue from below a pile of fashion magazines on the table.

'See these carpets—they are mine. And this mat—that's also one of mine.' I flicked the glossy pages, admiring the carpets and rugs manufactured by his company.

'I'm off to Frankfurt next week for the world carpet fair,' Vijay murmured, pushing his leg against mine.

I shifted away. 'What's wrong?' he said. 'Don't you like me?'

I stood up and looked down at him. 'I barely know you, Vijay,' I said sharply. He caught my hand.

'Oh come on, Ritu, you've come to my place, haven't you? Let's not waste time.' I sighed in resignation: *So much for him not getting the 'wrong' idea, the so-called evolution of men, notions on how men these days take the matter of consent seriously, how going to a man's house means nothing...*

'Let's eat first, I'm hungry. What are we eating?' I said desperately, pushing him away.

My lack of response to his overtures didn't go down well with Vijay. He banged down his glass on the table, and stormed off to the other room. A few moments later, he returned with a stack of menus.

'Take your pick,' he barked, throwing them at me.

I suggested a pepperoni pizza. A moment later, he refilled my glass with some more of the extra strong. I looked around for a potted plant I could water with it. But there was none. So there I was, stuck in a brothel-like apartment, with a narcissistic ex-model: *The worst beer on earth and an unkempt man by my side.* It was hardly a poetic moment.

'So do you have a girlfriend, Vijay?' I ventured.

He frowned in disbelief. 'Girlfriend? What's that? I've had one girlfriend in my whole life, when I was fifteen years old.'

'Why is that?' I asked.

'Who has girlfriends these days? All those how-are-you-doing calls, dinners, and the other shit of relationship, who needs that? There are enough women around who are ready to be with me when I need them,' he tossed out.

'Really?' I said disbelievingly. 'You just call your lady pals and they show up?'

'Depends,' he replied, impatiently, 'whether they are free, and in the mood.'

I mulled this over. 'I guess there are enough women around who are happy in a no-strings-attached relationship.'

'It's the best kind of deal there is. I give them a good time in and out of bed,' he said. 'What more could they want?'

Thankfully the pizza arrived, and I bit into a slice, wondering what kind of women considered Kingfisher Strong and pizza adequate incentive to get into bed with Vijay. Maybe the model factor swung the balance in his favour? Like it or not, he was like a lion, majestic-looking enough to attract whoever he wanted to his lair.

'Maybe,' I said. 'But that kind of relationship would never work for me.' I put down my plate decisively.

Vijay rolled his eyes and raised his eyebrows. 'That's just too bad for you... You don't know what you're missing out on.'

He fiddled around with some CDs, and chose one. 'I Wanna Love You' by Akon & Snoop Dog.

I feel you winding, grinding up on the floor, I know you see me lookin' at you and you already know I wanna love you, love you…

He came and sat down beside me and put his hand on my thigh.

'Come on, let me show you a good time,' he whispered, trying to bite my ear.

'A woman your age shouldn't play games. You shouldn't feel guilty or shy about wanting sex with me…I won't judge you,' he went on.

My head jerked back in surprise. 'What?'

'I know you want it even though you don't have the guts to ask for it,' he said, swaying to the music as he tried to pull me closer to him.

'No,' I said, pushing him away. 'I don't want it.'

~

My experience with Vijay taught me that the culture of consent is a lot more complicated than we imagine. It goes beyond the prevention of sexual assault. Male willingness to pay heed to the word 'No' is about respect and thoughtfulness. 'No' can mean many things: sorry, not now…I don't feel like it, or just NO, never.

Fortunately, I managed to strike up happy friendships with other younger men, that made up for the sour taste my brush with Vijay left in my mouth. There was 32-year-old Anirban, whom I met at a seminar on family planning. A thin, whimsical sort of fellow, he spoke with a clipped British accent acquired during his stint at the London School of Economics. Coincidentally, he lived in the lane opposite my place. We encountered each other at the Mother Dairy booth off and on, and one day he just dropped in at my place. It was fun being with him, and we struck up an easy friendship. He had none of the inhibitions of my generation of men, and was completely direct about his feelings. One day he told me he liked me. Just like that. I thanked him, and let him know that I didn't reciprocate his interest in the same way. Anirban looked a bit crestfallen but said it was 'cool'—he'd like to hang around with me, regardless. For a few days, I thought he was joking, since I'd never met a man who valued me enough to keep up the connection, unless sex was on the agenda.

This was the beginning of my first real friendship with a guy. It was the only time I managed to maintain a platonic, yet intimate relationship with a man I'd rejected romantically. Our relationship convinced me of the possibility of making friends with a man who had other ideas about me: surely we could go out for a meal or a movie once in a while?

Anirban would show up at my front door a couple of evenings a week, beer and momos in hand. We'd watch movies, listen to music and talk about our books (his reading list went from Camus to Ian McEwan), movies and dreams. Our relationship was unfettered by the constraints I normally felt around older men. There was no pressure to behave in any defined way, say anything I didn't mean or stress myself out looking after him.

Not long after we became friends, Anirban confessed he was on medication for bipolar disorder, and had tried to end his life on a couple of occasions. This made me nervous and wary of hurting him. But our friendship chugged on uneventfully, till he decided to immigrate to Australia.

~

Everyone says that female friendships are the bedrock of women's lives; that women friends compensate for many missing factors, including the absence of a husband or lover. But this hasn't proven true for me. My inner circle of female friends has always been small, and my attempts to enlarge it half-hearted. One reason is that I'm not extroverted. The other is that many aspects of femininity make me uncomfortable: the need for intimacy and constant connection, the compulsion to be nice and the tendency many women have to victimize themselves. The power they attribute to the men in their lives, scares me.

The women whose company I've enjoyed most are anti-establishment, by and large. They live as free women, even within traditional set-ups. Some have walked out of situations that trapped them, and are late bloomers. Their journeys to self-realization are wild and unconventional: they've chanted, meditated, danced and painted their way to new selves. There's K and M and A and C: women who wear skirts and dangling earrings, who enjoy being alone to an almost obsessive degree, and uphold freedom as their highest value. These quintessential wild women are unafraid to an extent that terrifies patriarchal society.

Another group of people I relate easily to is that of homosexual men. They have an appealing mix of masculine and feminine traits. Many are fantastic business managers, cooks, interior decorators, fashion designers, writers and dancers. My deep sense of affiliation with this group probably has something to do with their empathy and warmth, and also my own feelings of comfort in their company. They provide a safe space that is otherwise absent—both with heterosexual men, and in couples' gatherings.

~

But I did have the chance to test what being a cougar was like, on one occasion, when I summoned up the guts to embark on a romance with a much younger man. Sandeep was a journalist, a real bright spark who was always the centre of attraction at social gatherings. Striking up a relationship with him was a real stretch for me, since the rules were alien to me: stay 'cool', avoid rules and demands, and ensure that interactions never became too complicated or loaded.

Still, I decided to give it a go. After all, he seemed like a fully functional adult, who lived by himself. There was no mummy or daddy hovering around, and I was impressed with his kitchenette, equipped with pots and pans and a stove.

But I soon discovered that first impressions can be misleading. Sandeep regarded his life as a daily party: pizza and mutton rolls from the nearby dhaba were staples and the kitchenette was hardly used, nor was housekeeping one of his interests. Dust adhered to every surface in the flat, and it was best to avoid looking into his toilet bowl.

Yet, I couldn't resist playing Mummy: I'd change his sheets and carry over boxes of meat curry and mixed vegetables. I made him my Project Change, for a while. Since he was a couch potato, I nagged him to eat fresh food, go for a walk, sign up for a gym membership and take his vitamins.

He listened to it all good-humouredly. 'Hey thanks,' he'd say, opening the packet of Lay's sour onion chips that rested beside the plate of rice and curry I'd heated for him.

∼

After a couple of months of battling with his mess, I decided it was easier to leave the dishes and dirty clothes where they were, and avoid opening the fridge as I couldn't bear to look at the mould that encrusted the rubber lining.

Then, I considered moving the relationship into my space. But this didn't work because our lifestyles were so radically different. His was far more fun than mine. He kept company with all kinds of interesting people—filmmakers, musicians, writers and activists—who would come by to his place after 9 p.m. Stimulating conversations, music and booze made for great parties. Everything depended upon spontaneity though. Being an intrinsically over-involved and regulated human being, I liked advance plans. Sandeep, on the other hand, liked to call and say 'So what's up?' ten minutes before setting up a meeting.

In any case, there was no easy way for Sandeep's friends to breeze in and out of my place all night since my landlord was a nasty guy who kept an eye on comings and goings. My maid also sulked because there was such a mess of ash and dirty glasses to clear up every morning. Eventually, I opted out of his party routine. Functioning on six hours of sleep snatched after 2 a.m. after his gatherings broke up, was impossible.

I wondered how the cougar thing worked for other

women. How did they handle the stress associated with behaving like they were ten years younger than their chronological age? Aside from the mismatch in energy levels, there was the business of wrinkles and sagging body parts too. It must take a dedicated exercise routine and a generous budget for creams and beauty salons to stay in shape for a younger lover.

Makeup couldn't hide the creases around my eyes and neither a wonder bra nor compression underwear concealed my cellulite or the impact of gravity on my body. Looking at the young women in tiny blouses and mini-skirts who came and went from Sandeep's apartment, only added to my discomfort. 'You're very uptight,' he remarked, sensing my anxiety.

Our decision to part was mutual, and marked the end of my illusion about having a meaningful long-term relationship with a much younger man. What surfaced instead was the knowledge that I didn't want to mother a man ever again, or compromise myself to the degree that I'd done with Sandeep. This was the last time I tried to act younger than I was, just to fit into a mould cast by a romantic partner.

14

A Close Shave

Soon after this chapter in my life came to a close, I was distracted from romance by a series of unfortunate incidents. My C.R. Park apartment was burgled, in broad daylight. I came home from work at 5 p.m. one day, and found my front door wide open. A burglar had entered my place with a key, and made off with everything of value: savings I had carelessly stashed in my cupboard, bits of wedding jewellery, a camera, my laptop, even bottles of perfume.

Instinctively, I knew that the landlord's servant, B, was connected to the crime. He had access to my flat through the back door, which opened onto the terrace where his room was. I'd often spotted him lurking around my windows. Also, he had access to the landlord's spare key.

I made several trips to the local police station and met with inspectors and sub-inspectors in an attempt to have them conduct a proper investigation into the theft. Ironically, the head inspector of the police station was a woman. She walked about in tight khakis, her mouth a gash of maroon lipstick.

I launched into my tale of plunder, imagining she would sympathize with another woman's plight. She nodded a few times, appearing to take the matter seriously. For the next two days, the police came and went. They questioned my maid in a half-hearted manner and apprehended the landlord's domestic for a few hours. The landlord used all the clout he had to get B off the hook since he and his wife were utterly dependent on him.

Not long afterwards, someone smashed the windshield of my car. My feeling of being terrorized grew, but I told myself it was just an accident. Two days later, my rear view mirrors were stolen. Again, I filed a report at the police station. Again, no action was taken. The vandalism wouldn't end. Tyres were punctured and mudguards stolen. A month later, I was told that my case had been closed.

∼

Serendipitously, a family property in Greater Kailash-1 fell vacant. Unlike the previous two flats I'd lived in, this was large and spacious, like the houses of my childhood. There was a driveway to park my car, a room-cum-kitchenette set-up for a live-in domestic help, and a kitchen with space for both my Baby Belling ovens.

My friends and family gave me pieces of furniture to fill the spaces, and everything assumed its rightful place: soon I had a 'proper' house, with a dining table, a dressing table in my bedroom and a balcony with enough space for plants. I also had a full-time maid called Helen, who brewed ginger tea every morning and ensured I ate my meals on time.

The change in the quality of life was nothing short of miraculous. My sense of struggle diminished temporarily. What a relief to press the 'pause' button on writing my own script, and being the sole director and actor of my life! It was nearly a decade since I'd started my new life, and I couldn't recall a moment when I'd been able to get off the treadmill. Aside from my search for Mr Right, the search for a livelihood had consumed me more than I'd realized until this moment.

At this point, I had to face that my attempts to establish financial security for myself had failed. The longest period I'd managed to hold on to a job was four years. The rest of the time, I'd lived from article to article, project to project. 'Take it as it comes' was my motto.

Moving into this comfortable apartment was a real boon, since it meant I didn't have to worry about raising rent money, at least for the moment.

～

I kept up my coffee table conversations with men, though these were more occasional now. Every few months, I'd set up a meeting at Café Turtle, a quaint little bistro-style cafe above a bookshop in the N block market near where I lived. The coffee wasn't as fresh as Costa's, but the banana-caramel cake and glorious natural light made up for this lack. This time around, the coffee dates were more relaxed and fun than they'd been eight years earlier. Most of them were a dead-end romantically, but this didn't matter, since I wasn't as emotionally invested.

My new want list for a mate read something like this: he should be proactive and demonstrate his love with actions; he should have a steady personality, be financially secure, and enjoy travel, books and movies. Passion was highly overrated, I'd concluded, and abiding friendship and affection counted much more.

The only aspect of a romantic relationship I was still

befuddled about was what form it should take. The idea of marriage seemed almost ludicrous now. I doubted I'd be able to adjust to living with a man full-time. Why would I move into someone else's space when my own was so comfortable? I had nearly come to the conclusion that too much togetherness killed romance. Maybe living separately was the answer?

I was in this frame of mind when I first saw Suvir at a memorial service for a friend's father in the neighbourhood gurdwara. The service had ended and everyone was gathered for tea in the courtyard. I was about to bite into a plump samosa when I saw a lean, bearded man bend and feed a little girl spoonfuls of gulab jamun. When she finished eating, he took a napkin and gently wiped off the sticky syrup. I was mesmerized. He looked up for a brief moment and our eyes met. I turned away quickly, embarrassed at being caught staring at him.

I've always been a sucker for men who are hands-on fathers: they epitomize the New Age ideal of the sensitive, caring man. Young women are likely to laugh at me, since they expect nothing less from their men and can't even imagine a partner who doesn't share the load. Still, I can't resist making superheroes out of males who feed their kids and aren't too embarrassed to take them to the loo.

As luck would have it, I ran into the gurudwara daddy again, at a terrace party hosted by a friendly neighbour. Summer was on its way out, and a cool breeze heralded the onset of winter. It was the perfect season to sit outdoors. I could smell the aroma of kebabs as I climbed the three flights of stairs to the terrace garden. A glorious sight greeted me. Candles shimmered in corners and on tabletops, and for a moment, I felt like I was in fairyland. Almost miraculously, I came face to face with the man of the gulab-jamun moment. His face broke into a smile. 'Have we met before?'

I smiled self-consciously, wondering if I should mention where we'd first seen each other. So many years of navigating the world of South Delhi men had taught me to cover up some reactions, but clearly not well enough. 'Your eyes are a complete giveaway,' someone once told me. I blinked when I remembered this. But I needn't have worried, since the gurudwara daddy was obviously happy to see me. He put his hand out in greeting. 'I'm Suvir.' I clasped his hand, enjoying the sensation of warmth from his palm and the musky fragrance he exuded.

We chatted for a while: he said was a cardiologist at one of the top private hospitals in South Delhi. I told him I was a health journalist. His interest perked. 'Really? Do you have any background in health?' I told him about my degree in microbiology, and work in health communications. 'The combination works when it comes to writing on health topics,' I explained. He shook his head approvingly. 'Sounds like you're on a good track.'

We got into a discussion on arterial blockages, cardiac defibrillators, murmurs and heart transplants. The thought that he made a living from fixing people's hearts made me warm to him, and the feeling of connectedness between us was palpable. But we were interrupted by our hostess, accompanied by a man. 'Talking shop as usual, Dr Singh,' she said jokingly, 'I want you to take a minute off, and meet another neighbour.'

I stood back, admonishing myself for my interest in

him. *He's a married man... Not available...* The thought of his 'wife' made my stomach sink. I looked around to see if there was any woman in his vicinity who had a proprietorial air. Only the hostess was by his side though. Once again, Suvir caught me gazing at him. I looked away abruptly, and went off to get a kebab. A few seconds later, he wandered over to me. 'Have you tried this?' I said, waving my mutton roll at him, to distract myself from unsteady feelings, '...it's amazing.'

He seemed amused by my hungry enthusiasm. 'Yes,' he said, 'everything from this caterer's kitchen is superb...he runs one of those famous Old Delhi Indian food set-ups.' Suvir reached out to dab my chin with a napkin. I stood transfixed, feeling like a messy child. I always managed to drop food all over myself. 'It was just about to ruin your lovely purple blouse,' he said, by way of explanation. 'Thanks,' I murmured, uncertain about whether the intimacy bred by his touch was welcome or not.

'So do you use this caterer's services often?' I said, trying to steer the interaction into a safe zone.

A shadow crossed his face. 'No, not really...I don't entertain much,' he said, dipping his roll into mint chutney before taking a neat bite. 'But I've eaten his fare at friends' parties, and it's always first-class.' He stroked his immaculate beard. 'How about you, Ritu, do you have a lot of parties, socialize much?'

'No, I don't have too many parties,' I said contemplatively, '...and when I do, they are always small. Crowds scare me...also, I enjoy doing the cooking myself, so...'

He looked impressed. 'That's great—you're a woman with many talents. Health writer and cooking expert. Oh, by the way my mother also believes in making everything herself. Every single jar of jam and chutney in our house has been made by her.'

'That sounds familiar,' I said. 'All the women in my family are crazy about food—we bake all our own cakes and spend all our time discussing recipes.'

An expression of rapt admiration spread over Suvir's face. 'So what kind of food do you cook best?' he asked, moving closer to me.

'Anything that comes out of an oven,' I enthused. 'Cakes, pies, muffins, baked chicken, lasagna.' I paused. 'But I have no idea how to cook a good Indian meal.'

'So Western continental, hanh?' he said. 'That's my favourite kind of cuisine.'

'Is it?' I said, wondering if this was just a line. 'What's your favourite restaurant then?'

He responded immediately. 'Big Chill, I guess—the kids also love it. Every single item on their menu—from the pizzas to the grilled fish and cheesecake—is always good.'

I took a deep breath to quell the feelings of irrational disappointment that arose in my chest at the knowledge that he had kids. What did I expect? I'd seen him feeding his little girl, hadn't I? Still, I couldn't control my regret that he wasn't available.

Suvir didn't appear to be constrained by his family obligations though. 'Let's get together for a meal sometime,' he said, asking for my number and handing me his card. I mumbled a vague reply and tucked the card into the recesses of my bag. The thought that he would call and invite me out for one of those family dinners—wife, kids and maybe even mother—made me feel despondent. I told myself to forget it: the chances of hearing from him were slim, and there was nothing to worry about.

∼

But Suvir did call, a week later. We discussed the goings-on of our lives, and then he said: 'Since you like kebabs, I thought we could go to a new kebab place I discovered recently.'

I was startled, even though I'd sensed his interest in me. He seemed like a solid sort of guy, a respected doctor, and family man—hardly the kind who would cheat on his wife or seek an extra-marital dalliance. But then, who knew? The truth was that appearances were deceptive.

'What about your wife?' I blurted out. There were sounds of throat clearing.

'Relax,' he said. 'There's no wife.'

Suvir, or Dr Suvir Singh as his patients knew him, said he was recently divorced and shared custody of his two daughters with his wife.

'You have such a hectic schedule,' I ventured. 'How do you manage to look after them?'

He told me that he lived in the apartment above his parents', and his mother helped him with taking care of the kids. Being a single father in such a situation wasn't too hard.

'What about your son—does he live with you?' he asked, curiously.

I scraped my fork desolately across my empty plate, and tried to explain my son's new living arrangements. Last month L had moved to a new school, and needed to sign up for a regular bus route. There was no way he could keep moving between his father's place and mine.

'Whatever is best for you,' I said to L, with a heavy heart. We both knew the answer already. G's home was closer to the school, and fell on the bus route. So, from being with me most of the week, L now stayed with me primarily on weekends.

I let my child go, with a mixture of sadness and understanding. Since the time I'd struck out on my own, I'd been careful to avoid playing the 'poor me' card with him. I'd seen enough unhealthy relationships between single mothers and their sons, and was determined to avoid using my child to fill any emotional void in my life. Women without partners—and those in unhappy marriages—are especially guilty of trying to turn their sons into surrogate husbands. I didn't want to fall into this trap.

~

Suvir and I got involved a few weeks after the kebab evening. He had a strong, authoritative manner and instinctively took charge of situations. Chivalry may be long gone for some, but not for me: I enjoyed the way he opened car doors, inquired about my health daily, and delivered on every single promise he made. When we went out, he'd come to my front door to pick me up, and when he dropped me off, he'd wait till I was back inside my home, before driving off. He was almost primal in his protectiveness. In comparison, the nonchalance of other men appeared boorish.

Also, he did all the manly stuff I hated, taking over

household repairs and bank jobs. Despite his work at the hospital, Suvir did whatever he could to make my life easier. He wore down my attitude of self-reliance, urging me to depend upon him for small things. He ensured that all the electrical sockets in my house worked, and that my medicine cabinet was well stocked with Combiflam. Eventually, I dropped my guard and stopped trying to maintain my 'I can manage everything myself' stance.

We fell into a zone of comfort quickly, maybe too quickly. Perhaps this was because both of us were lonely. Also, so many years of searching for Mr Right had dampened my exploratory spirit. The mere thought of falling into yet another tedious courtship game was exhausting. Despite my emancipation, I wanted to stop holding back, and love fully. I wanted to be nurtured by a partner who'd regard my interests as important as his own. Falling into lust, time and again, was so easy. But finding solid ground was another matter entirely.

Apart from his more obvious charismatic qualities, Suvir was rare in that he reciprocated my level of attentiveness. He remembered exactly how much sugar I liked in my tea, which brand of toothpaste I favoured, and when I needed a nap. He was one of those guys who would water my plants daily, if I asked him to. This very quality—his willingness to engage in tasks typically considered female domain—led me to imagine that he was different from other men of my generation.

So far, most of the 60s- and 70s-born men I'd met seemed stuck in a time warp. They were comfortable in traditional male roles, as breadwinners and problem fixers, but inflexible otherwise. Apart from a few tokenistic gestures—picking up groceries on an odd day, hanging their wet towels outside after their baths, or ordering pizza for the family—these guys were singularly devoted to acting out their masculinity in the way that their fathers did.

Suvir seemed different. In some way, he was every woman's mother. Meeting him revived my faith in romance, for the first time since my relationship with Vikram had ended.

~

In the beginning, we kept our relationship secret. 'It's better that way, at least till we are sure,' he said, and I agreed. The thought of bringing our families into the situation so early didn't arise. Plus, he and I were having so much fun. We tried out all the new restaurants in town, worked out together at the gym, and watched lots of films together. I loved cooking for him, and he quickly became a fan of my chocolate fudge cakes and chicken quiches.

But then one day, Suvir suggested we 'test the ground' with his daughters.

'Let's go to Big Chill together,' he said. 'Why don't you bring your son, too?'

I agreed, with some misgivings, terrified about the change this move was designed to introduce into our equation. But there was no way to evade the full picture forever.

We spent a noisy evening together, bonding over pizzas and ice cream. He invited another couple and their kids, and introduced me as a journalist who'd been in touch with him for an article about heart disease. It didn't matter anyway, since conversation was impossible.

Suvir was in his element with his daughters, and fell into the father role with L almost immediately. 'What's your favourite pizza, beta?' he quizzed, putting his arm around L's shoulders.

Later that night I praised him for his caring attitude. 'You are such a great father,' I said, feeling almost tearful as I said this; deep down I felt that his love for his children would always win over any feelings he had for me.

But the single area I knew nothing about was why his marriage had broken up. Every time I pushed for information, Suvir was evasive. 'Incompatibility,' he said dismissively. 'She was unfit to be either a wife or a mother.'

His vague explanation left my curiosity unsatisfied, but he wouldn't say anything more. I told myself that divorce was obviously a bigger aberration for him than for other men I had known. His reluctance to talk about his broken relationship was linked to his sense of failure. Despite this rationalization, I still felt uneasy about not knowing the truth.

Till that evening, it had been easy to pretend that he had no baggage, and was completely free to start a new life with me. In the following weeks, I began to picture what a permanent relationship with Suvir would mean. My illusions of independence slowly vanished. Moving in with him involved interacting with his parents everyday, since his apartment was just above theirs. The proximity, as he kept reminding me, had been a lifesaver after the divorce.

'My mother's presence has been a godsend,' he declared. 'She's around for the kids more than their own mother was.'

It was clear that he held his mother in high regard for the sacrifices she had made for him. 'She had to drop out of all the ladies' groups she's a member of, give up her weekly kitty, and her trips to the Golden Temple too,' he told me.

I was nonplussed, both at his mother's martyrdom, and at his ready acceptance of her surrender. For me, the self-sacrificing wife and mother that Hindi movies and TV serials projected as role models were highly overrated. 'That must be very hard for her,' I commented. 'Giving up a lifestyle she enjoyed to take care of little children, at her age.'

He looked grimly at me and shook his head. 'Not at all. My mother doesn't mind—she knows it's the right thing to do, they are her grandchildren after all.'

I was nonplussed at his apparently regressive stance, and wondered if he expected me to assume the same role as his mother, if we got married? Would I have to give up my work and other activities to look after his kids too?

Perhaps I had been naïve to assume that Suvir was attracted to my independence, and free spirit? Maybe he imagined this aspect of my personality was fleeting; that I'd mould myself into the kind of woman he seemed to idealize, once we settled into a permanent relationship. It was ironic how I was up against the same wall once again, wondering about how to conform to a man's expectations of me.

～

Nearly a year after we met, Suvir started talking about marriage. 'It's time to settle down, don't you think? I mean, we've known each other for nearly a year, and I love you,' he said, reaching for my hand. I hugged him, struggling with feelings of excitement and confusion. A part of me was elated at the fresh chance to 'settle down'. After all, how many women in India got the chance to remarry at the ripe old age of forty-five? Indeed, it was gratifying to be with a man who was a good human being, and regarded me as a potential life partner—a woman fit to mother his children and support him.

Yet, I couldn't ignore the sense of foreboding in my gut at the thought of becoming a wife and stepmother. It was ironic how I was being tested, yet again. Nearly a decade after I had turned down Vikram's proposal, I was confronted with the same dilemma all over again: should I marry a man with children? Was it worth sacrificing my freedom to be in a marriage? I tried to buy some time by telling Suvir we needed to think through the details first, of what it would mean to set up home together.

～

Once the intention of a relationship changes, so do the dynamics.

Despite our somewhat unresolved conversation about the direction of our relationship, our daily interactions changed. Suvir's behaviour became more purposeful, and less spontaneous. He announced that it was time for me to make a visit to his home, and meet his parents too.

'Mummy will probably come across as snooty in the beginning—she takes some time to warm up to people—but I know she'll love the idea of having another woman around the house.'

Instead of feeling pleased at the thought of meeting his mother, I was dismayed. The prospect of having to interact with her on a daily basis was daunting. Middle-aged me had a fierce need to maintain my boundaries, more clarity about what I liked and disliked, and even less capacity to adapt to other people's expectations than I'd had in my youth.

But nothing could stop Suvir from planning our future. 'You haven't seen the house yet, but I'm guessing you'll need another cupboard in the bedroom,' he said, 'maybe one in the kitchen too—for your baking equipment.'

I feigned interest, while he continued to describe the layout of his apartment, my future home. The image of me wearing an apron, stirring a pot on the stove of an unfamiliar kitchen popped into my head. I stirred and stirred, but the food in the pot kept solidifying and soon, the smell of charring permeated the air...

I ignored my misgivings, and allowed myself to get swept up in the illusion of a new life. It was easy to fall into all the trappings of this promise. So I went along, trying my best to respond to the issues Suvir kept raising. The first one centered around my wardrobe, which he felt needed an upgrade: there would be lots of official dinners to attend, meetings with school principals and other events like kirtans at his parents' home.

'Let's go clothes shopping,' he suggested. 'We'll pretend we're enacting *Pretty Woman*...you're Julia Roberts, and I'm Richard Gere, with a smaller wallet though,' he joked. I sighed, thinking enviously of Julia's gorgeous body. My own had expanded considerably over the past few months.

So one Saturday, we headed to a mall with a range of clothing stores. Though I usually shopped for Western wear from Marks & Spencer, Suvir decided that I needed salwar kameezes and sarees instead.

'Indian clothes suit you so much better,' he declared,

waiting outside the changing room for me to model each garment.

After we'd settled on the sarees and salwar kameezes, I wandered off to the Levis shop for some jeans. I picked a few pairs off the rack, and took them to the trial room. A moment later, there was a tap on the door.

'It's me,' he said. 'Aren't you going to model them for me?'

I emerged a few moments later. 'So, what do you think?'

His brows furrowed when he saw me. 'Not that pair,' he said, decisively. 'You need a style that emphasizes your waist and shrinks your hips.'

I'd asked for an opinion but this was fashion advice I could do without. Before I could retort, he disappeared. When he reappeared, he was holding a pile of garments, all either blue or purple.

'You need to throw away all those black things you keep wearing,' he said, thrusting the pile of blouses and skirts at me. 'Now try these out.'

Though we left the mall with two large bags of clothes, all I could think about at that moment was how to get away from Suvir. It was ironic how the very aspect of his personality that had attracted me in the first place—his authoritative manner and tendency to take over situations—was also his downfall. As far as I was concerned, the moment the 'don't do this, don't do that' begins in a relationship, trouble isn't far behind.

After the shopping expedition, Suvir announced that I needed to lose some weight. He suggested I give up hard-crust bread and mangoes (two of my favourite foods) in a bid to lose the five extra pounds of flesh that had settled on my hips and stomach.

'Just imagine how sexy you'll look without the flab,' he said, hastening to remind me that the weight loss would also improve my heart health.

I frowned. 'Oh come on, Suvir…I'm hardly a contender for Miss India, am I? And my heart is in great shape, thanks.'

~

This was just the beginning of a new, unnerving phase in our relationship. Suvir's proprietary interest in me soared with every passing day.

'So do you believe in monogamy?' he said one night. 'You've obviously been around with many men…and before we marry, I think it's my right to know all about your past.'

'There's nothing to worry about, Suvir,' I said as evenly as I could. 'The past is just that…the past.'

He glared at me, dissatisfied with my response. I felt like throwing the glass of water I was drinking at him.

The next day, he got going on the subject of household expenses.

'My ex wasted a lot of money on fruit and veggies,' he said. 'Instead of buying them from Mother Dairy, she insisted it should all come from some fancy organic shop.'

I nodded, despite my growing feeling of foreboding. My interest in vegetable and fruit shopping, like many other aspects of domestic life, was limited. But Suvir was like a bull, charging from one matter to another.

'So, what are your monthly beauty parlour expenses?' he asked.

'What?' I shot back, unsure about whether I had heard right or not.

He looked impatient. 'My ex-wife went to get her hair and nails done twice a week,' he explained. 'This was in addition to other treatments like facials and so on, so I had to give her at least fifteen thousand a month for this. I need to know how much your beauty routine costs.'

I was dumbfounded. The reality of what I was getting into was unavoidable. If I married Suvir, I would have to discuss every single move I made with him: whether I was going for a facial exfoliation, mani-pedi or whatever else. How mortifying!

Here I was, an independent 45-year-old woman, actually contemplating making a decision that would limit, rather than expand my life. The harder I tried to hang on to the rosy picture of coupledom I'd created in my head, the louder the noise in my brain became.

My terror at the prospect of being trapped in the wife-children-in-law cage interfered with my work and sleep. On the surface, life seems better for women. The 'New Indian Woman' is portrayed as urban, working, self-confident, physically and socially mobile, with a cosmopolitan outlook. But does the man who embraces her fully, really exist? Of course, I understood the mindset of men my age, since we'd grown up at the same time. But getting them to budge on their often outdated views, relate differently, or adopt a more flexible role in relationships, was another matter. The larger question was whether I could live with someone shackled by outdated notions of masculinity, who thrived on machismo?

∼

Divine intervention changed the direction of our lives.

Just a month after he'd broached the topic of marriage, Suvir suggested we discuss our career plans for the next year, so that we could plan 'our' domestic schedule more effectively.

'Also, what are we going to do about your work timings?' he said, looking at me questioningly.

'What do you mean?' I said. 'What have my work timings got to do with anything?'

He shook his head. 'You'll be in charge of the kids, remember?'

'Sure,' I said tersely. 'But my work timings are inflexible.'

His face acquired a steely expression. 'Look, Ritu, the kids haven't ever had a proper mother,' he said. 'Niloufer used to loll around in bed all the time, and watch TV when they came home from school. She wouldn't even serve them lunch herself.'

'But you have a maid, don't you?' I retorted. 'Surely she can give the kids their lunch?'

'Don't be silly, Ritu,' was his response. 'A good mother supervises her children's meals—how else can she ensure they are eating properly? In fact, one of the main reasons I was attracted to you was because you are such a good cook. I knew you'd be good for the kids.'

I shrugged, fighting back the sinking sensation in my stomach. 'Yes, I love good food and cooking, Suvir. But that's a hobby, not something that comes at the expense of my work. I thought you knew I wasn't going to give up my work. Surely you understood this? I will help with the kids, of course,' I countered, desperate for some sign that Suvir wasn't as regressive as he appeared to be, and that the discussion would end here.

Suvir was oblivious to my distress, and just kept shaking his head grimly.

'Unbelievable,' he muttered. 'I expected more from you. I'm not looking for some help with my girls, I'm looking for a woman who will mother them properly... the way my mother cares for them,' his tone and expression conveying his distaste for women like me.

'My mother made so many sacrifices to raise me right. She stood waiting for me at the busstop in the sun every day to escort me home from school, and then fed me the food she had cooked with her own hands. No one can ever match her...'

I sat down on the bed, and covered my face in resignation. Suvir sat beside me, and tried to put his arm around my shoulders. But I wasn't comforted, I was exhausted. So, I took his hand and said, 'I'm sorry—it's just not going to work.'

15
A New Beginning

Romantic breakups aren't always devastating. The ability to bounce back increases, as your comfort with your own company grows. There are familiar routines to fall back upon, predictable pleasures like the cup of coffee brewed in your own pot and the morning walk in the green and peaceful park around the corner.

Of course, I missed Suvir's warm presence in my life. More than that, the ending of our relationship broke the spell that put me on the romantic trail in the first place. It was time to face that Mr Right didn't exist, and that there was no Mr Wrong either. My unrealistic expectations from romantic relationships were apparent. I didn't need to look any further to realize that I wouldn't find all the qualities I was looking for in one man. And that gender equality couldn't be reduced to who did the housework or who looked after the kids. Women could only realize their own dreams in the company of men who were intrinsically kind and considerate to them. Being unselfish isn't easy, and maybe that's why it's so hard for many of us to forge meaningful intimate relationships.

These realizations led to a slow dissolution of my fierce attachment to the idea of romantic love; along with the impulse to float along aimlessly with any man who attracted me. Having spent so much time pondering and plotting my love life, initially I was a bit lost minus a love focus. But after my hankering for romance abated, I began experiencing a different sort of contentment, the kind that depended more on Dominos pepperoni pizza and a good film, than a man. Though the desire to get involved arose off and on, I didn't act on it, and discovered it disappeared as quickly as it had appeared. Maybe this had something to do with my changing hormone levels, since I was now officially in the 'pre-menopausal' phase of my life.

In any case, it was time to face that I didn't want to slip back into a traditional relationship with any man again. Having turned down two marriage proposals since the beginning of my romantic quest, I knew there was no point in venturing down that path ever again. I really wasn't interested in taking on the role of domestic manager, or stepmother. Perhaps it was best to give up the traditional notion of family altogether?

To me, mid-life was the time to live in a more authentic manner, and called for new relationship dynamics. For women especially, this is a phase of self-actualization, and any relationship that isn't supportive of their emancipation isn't worth hanging on to. Why tie up energy in trying to maintain a difficult romantic endeavour? The very thought of 'working on' any romantic relationship was hard to stomach.

Funnily enough, statistics showed that I wasn't alone in my thinking; that much younger women were already thinking along these lines. More Indian women today are choosing actively to bend rigid traditional norms by refusing to 'settle' for marriage. Social commentators say that financial independence has bred a new generation of thirty-something women more keen on enjoyment and freedom than marriage, in-laws and babies. Modern love seems to have created a disinclination to marry, and women are entering into a variety of social arrangements in lieu of marriage: choosing boyfriends/man-friends, 'friends with benefits' and live-in relationships instead.

Living alone is listed by *Time* magazine, as the foremost idea to change and shape our lives. Indeed, this has become one of the most rapidly increasing social trends globally. Since the time I rented my first apartment, there was a 40 per cent increase in the number of single women in India. According to 2011 census data, there were around 73 million unmarried, divorced, separated and widowed women in the country, constituting 21 per cent of India's population. And the rise of single women in the age group of 20-29 was the highest at 68 per cent, said a 2014 article in the online magazine *India Spend*. Sociologists described single women as an 'exploding demographic segment that's etching their own rules.'

The latter part of this statement is not entirely true. Sure, it's less of a social taboo to be single, but that doesn't make life any easier. In reality, single women know how tenuous their rights are. They may or may not inherit property, just as they may or may not get a landlord to rent them a place. In the workplace, they still earn less than men doing the same job, and often struggle to prove they are as competent. Living alone is harder work for single women than men, since women aren't taken seriously by insurance agents, water meter readers, bank managers, electricians, building contractors, and the like—in all of these interactions, 'being a man' still makes a difference.

Many years of living by myself has made me increasingly aware of the restraints, and opportunities, that come with it. My personal freedom and solitude are of great value to me, and I'm supremely grateful that I found the courage to be autonomous at a late stage of my life. Along the way, I've reconnected with my ex, G, and we've developed a new relationship, and appreciation of each other.

We live in separate houses, dine together a few times a week, go on a couple of holidays with our son every year, and enjoy spending time with family and friends. Everyone tells me that our relationship is a miracle—how often does a woman reunite with a man she has been separated from for over a decade?

∼

The energy I expended in romantic pursuit was suddenly free, so I cultivated a lush terrace garden, baked a hundred cupcakes for a friend's Diwali party, and reread every single book written by Anita Brookner. Then, I decided to springclean and renovate my home, and ended up browsing the lanes of Chandni Chowk to buy fabric for new curtains and sofa covers.

A new opportunity to become a health columnist for a newspaper arose, and this opened up the world of medicine and health for me in a bigger way, leading to interactions with top doctors and scientists. I was invited to all kinds of workshops and lectures, and learned all about new healing modalities. I spent a week doing Osho meditations at Rajneesh's famous commune in Pune, picked up an esoteric therapy called theta healing from a UK-based practitioner, took a two-day course in spiritual belly dance from a practitioner trained in

Iran, and improved my posture via the famed Alexander Technique. At some point, I also learned karate, Sivananda Yoga and creative dance therapy and became friends with an American dancer called Zuleikha, who taught me dance movements that released the tightness in my back and neck.

Most exciting of all was a three-week course I undertook, in massage therapies. Advertised as a 'bodywork' course in a popular health magazine, the massage therapies workshop called for spending three weeks in a remote part of Goa, and learning different massage techniques, with a group of people. Funnily enough, my mother spotted the advert and suggested I go for it, since I loved massage so much. The problem was that the class was a mixed one, so participants would have to practice on both men and women.

I decided to write to the lady leading the course—a well-known American practitioner of energy medicine—requesting an exemption from practicing massage on men: *I really want to take your course. But I'm not comfortable doing massage on strange men, so is it okay if I stick to a female partner during sessions?*

The teacher's response was no-nonsense, somewhat racist, and exactly what I needed to shake off my doubts: *You Indian women need to get over your body hang-ups. If you want to get a certificate, you'll need to work on men and women in the class. No exceptions will be made.*

So, I took a deep breath and made my bookings. Two weeks later, I reached the guesthouse in South Goa, mentally prepared to suffer the embarrassment and discomfort I expected to feel when it came to massaging the body of a man who was a perfect stranger. Our teacher was a plump, straight-talking American woman who announced that I was the first 'middle-class Indian Hindu woman' to have signed up with her to learn massage therapies.

'You're the first Indian lady who doesn't consider it below your dignity to massage someone,' she said with some asperity, 'so consider yourself a radical.'

For four hours a day, I stood in my shorts, dripping with sweat and pummelling the limbs, bellies and backs of men and women on massage tables. By the evening, I was unable to distinguish the body parts from their owners. Fingers, toes, legs, arms, feet and hands assumed an identity all of their own. Once I began on a massage, my mind switched off and my hands just seemed to move of their own volition, kneading knots of tension, sliding over bones and muscles and exploring lumps and bumps.

As I poured oil over the plump, hairy shoulders of a supine coursemate, I wondered what I'd been so worried about. Neither he nor any of the other guys who'd lain on my massage table attracted or threatened me in any way: there was a pot-bellied astrologer from Lucknow whose flesh jiggled even before I touched him; a stiff-necked businessman from Mumbai who shrieked when I pressed down on his shoulders; and a benign-looking monk with a toned tummy, who was too virtuous to be sexy.

My nonchalance was a source of wonder. Here I was, handling a bunch of barebodied men with utter disdain. I felt sure and steady on my feet. My breath came calm and easy. All of a sudden, I realized I was free.

∼

Love After Love

The time will come
when, with elation
you will greet yourself arriving
at your own door, in your own mirror
and each will smile at the other's welcome,
and say, sit here. Eat.
You will love again the stranger who was your self.
Give wine. Give bread. Give back your heart
to itself, to the stranger who has loved you
all your life, whom you ignored
for another, who knows you by heart.
Take down the love letters from the bookshelf,
the photographs, the desperate notes,
peel your own image from the mirror.
Sit. Feast on your life.

Derek Walcott from
Collected Poems 1948-1984